LIVE
BIG!

KATIE BRAZELTON PHD, MDIV, MA

Bestselling Author and Life Coach
Founder, Life Purpose Coaching Centers International®

LIVE BIG!

10 LIFE COACHING TIPS for LIVING LARGE, PASSIONATE DREAMS

HOWARD BOOKS
A DIVISION OF SIMON & SCHUSTER, INC.

NEW YORK NASHVILLE LONDON TORONTO SYDNEY

Published by Howard Books, a division of Simon & Schuster, Inc.
1230 Avenue of the Americas, New York, NY 10020
www.howardpublishing.com

Live Big! © 2009 by Katie Brazelton

Life Purpose Coach® and Life Purpose Coaching Centers International® are registered trademarks. LaserCoaching℠ is a service mark of Life Purpose Coaching Centers International®.

In association with Nancy Jernigan and Hidden Value Group.

Library of Congress Cataloging-in-Publication Data
Brazelton, Katie, 1950–
Live big! : 10 life coaching tips for living large, passionate dreams / Katie Brazelton.
p. cm.
1. Life skills. 2. Quality of life. 3. Conduct of life. 4. Personal coaching. I. Title.
HQ2037.B735 2010
248.8'4—dc22
2009032143

ISBN: 1-978-4391-3560-0

10 9 8 7 6 5 4 3 2 1

HOWARD colophon is a registered trademark of Simon & Schuster, Inc.

Manufactured in the United States of America

For information regarding special discounts for bulk purchases, please contact: Simon & Schuster Special Sales at 1-866-506-1949 or business@simonandschuster.com.

The Simon & Schuster Speakers Bureau can bring authors to your live event. For more information or to book an event, contact the Simon & Schuster Speakers Bureau at 1-866-248-3049 or visit our website at www.simonspeakers.com.

Edited by Between the Lines
Cover design by Stephanie Walker
Interior design by Davina Mock-Maniscalco
Scrapbook page illustrations by Jason Snyder
Author photo by Katie Keller and Sue Foley Photography

To my incredible Life Purpose Coach students and grads,
who dream and pray with me about opening
more coed coaching centers worldwide.

Especially to the eight coaches who have allowed me to share
their testimonies in this book: Darlene Lund, Kristi Olson,
Judy Grandstrand, Jamie Beran, Natasha Swanepoel,
Mary Kay Moore, Michelle Cabell, and Joyce Meekins.

Contents

Preface

BEFORE WE DIVE IN TO TALK ABOUT HUGE HOPES AND daring dreams, I want to pause for a moment and make sure that we actually have our eyes set on our only real hope for the future. That can be none other than God, the One who holds our future in His hands. If the greatest desire of our heart is to know Him more intimately and love Him more dearly, we will bow to worship Him with the surrendered actions of our lives, fulfilling the incomparable destiny He assigned us before the world was formed. It is only then that we will truly *Live Big!*

Introduction

IMAGINE THAT YOU AND I ARE BEING PAMPERED IN FIRST class, relaxing comfortably on an afternoon flight to your favorite world-class resort. As we gaze out the airplane window, it seems as though we're floating through an endless sea of marshmallow clouds, soaring together through the heavens. Up here, dreams somehow seem crystal clear. I think it's because we can pretend we've risen above the rough, mountainous terrain of life and can look down on our hills and valleys, seeing events from a fresh perspective.

From this bird's-eye view, glance down at what is below: your daily routine, closest relationships, untapped potential, and countless opportunities. Let this vantage point help you set your sights on a passionate megadream and an inspiring hope for the future!

I would not dare to author a book on such an important topic as Living Big without practicing what I preach. So, as I write this, I am on a flight to Hawaii (I wish it were first class) for an extended stay to consider living there indefinitely. I was raised in Hawaii and the Marshall Islands in a navy family, so the tropical breeze has always been alluring to me. Might this be where I will plant another Life Purpose Coaching Center . . . or find the time to launch my long-dreamed-of radio show . . . or finish this book? I don't know the answers to those questions, but I do know that I can't fail, because this is simply an experiment, with memories waiting to be made. I'm not going to rush the process or force a decision, only enjoy the journey to yea or nay. There is no right or wrong way to dream.

Well, actually, I do believe there's one wrong way, and that is to let the dream stagnate without taking any action!

I am embarking on this time of exploration because I am in a new season of my life, formally ending two decades of single parenting. My son recently accepted an out-of-state job promotion, taking his sweet wife and my two young grandsons with him. Shortly thereafter, my daughter announced her engagement, which means she, too, will be moving away from our home area. In the blink of an eye, without my permission, I have been thrust into a new chapter of my life. On one hand, I am sad and fearful. On the other hand, now I have no more excuses for not doing whatever I want, which is another way of saying "whatever I feel God is calling me to do next."

I am operating in a spirit of supersized living right now, and not just because I may soon be draped in large muumuus, walking barefoot to the local market to buy macadamia-nut chocolates, and blatantly enticing my family with extended holiday vacations in paradise.

Dreaming in high definition and surround sound—and then taking appropriate steps to live those dreams—is what this book is all about. You may not have a burning desire to move to a distant land, but what do you want out of life? Are you a student anxiously finishing college? A young mom who's busy raising twins? An overseas missionary on a brand-new assignment? A career woman vying for an enviable position? A widow with only a few pressing obligations? Regardless of your role in life, you and I have a few things in common:

- We love to dream.
- God designed us to dream.
- And there's no day like today to start discovering God's best!

I need you to know that I'm not so far up in the clouds that I am unaware of your everyday realities. Life has prepared me well to be your Life Coach. I have a testimony of brokenness, and I'm honored to help you dream. Check out what I call "My 7 Big D's"—events that shaped me for nearly twenty years.

My 7 Big D's

1982	Barely survived a serious, four-month *depression*.
1986	Devastated by a totally unexpected *divorce*.
1988	Confused about having to rewrite my *doctoral dissertation*.

1990	Deeply saddened by the *death* of my ex-husband.
1991	Angered by a corporate *downsizing*, which left me laid off just days after buying a home.
1993	Terrified by a *dating* incident.
2001	Shocked by the *death of my dream* when my first book contract was canceled due to budget cuts after 9/11.

What does this list tell you, other than that I must have built up a lot of stamina by now? It says that you can trust me to understand what you're going through and to tell it like it is when I coach you—without skirting around the issues. I care deeply about making sure you don't get stuck in the quagmire of life, as I did too many times.

These chapters will take you on a journey to find what you're really jazzed about—what makes you smile, laugh, play, sing, and dance. It's time to daydream about the adventure God has in store for you!

Amos 4:13 tells us that God reveals His thoughts to us: "He who forms the mountains, who creates the wind, and who reveals his thoughts to mortals, who turns dawn to darkness, and treads on the heights of the earth—the LORD God Almighty is his name." We want to do whatever it takes to be ready for that revelation.

As your Life Coach, I will come alongside you like a Barnabas (a name that Acts 4:36 tells us means "son of encourage-ment"). We will enjoy life-changing chats about *you*, stealing precious moments within your hectic schedule. I know how hard it is for you to find time for a conversation about your leg-acy, your destiny, your divine urge. As you are able to sneak away from your daily routine, it will be my job and my joy to sit with you and draw out of you the distinct calling God laid on your heart eons ago, before you were ever born. And then, equally important, we will put baby steps in place to help you live out your exciting, God-designed purpose, which has long been the desire in your soul even if it has lain dormant.

This book is loaded with modern, true stories of everyday saints, Bible character parallels, inspirational quotes, some of my favorite Scripture verses, heartfelt prayers, ten coaching tips, forty action steps, reflection questions, and practical ex-ercises with sample answers from my own life to trigger your thinking. (Don't miss the Web downloads, too, which are my special gift to you!) You will hear from real women—stu-dents, wives, mothers, a widow, career women, church staff members—who all have tremendous testimonies to share. I urge you to break all of the normal book-reading rules and jump into the chapters in any sequence you please. Did you know that doing the unexpected can change your perspective, which will then cause you to see your world through new eyes?

I've chosen these particular topics for us to explore in detail as we discover what it takes to *Live Big!*

1. Face Your Fears
2. Learn to Exhale
3. Honor Your Deepest Longings
4. Don't Ever Give Up
5. Use Your Past for Good
6. Expect Miracles
7. Forgive Someone
8. Eat Dessert First
9. Ask Jesus for Vision
10. Capture Your *Live Big!* Dream

I can't help but think: *If only someone had told me that!* or *Why didn't I learn that in school?* Frankly, I feel there ought to be a law mandating that schools teach us to be tenacious, forgiving, and courageous. We need classes at church that help us reach for our dreams, expect miracles, focus forward, and breathe calmly through adversity. But most important, we must learn how to play and to stop taking ourselves so seriously and to start cherishing God's incredibly specific plan for our lives. In this way, we address the habits that help us attract or sabotage God's boldest wishes for us.

> Since we are surrounded by such a great cloud of witnesses, let us throw off everything that hinders and the sin that so easily entangles. And let us run with perseverance the race marked out for us.
>
> Hebrews 12:1

Each of the ten coaching tips will give you a broader, richer understanding of how to run and finish the race well.

You probably picked up this book because you want to travel boldly down the path to purpose and fulfillment, yet perhaps you've lost sight of your dreams, hopes, and longings—possibly because of regrets, exhaustion, stubbornness, fears, sins, and so on. We're all burdened with something. You want to bring glory to God with your life, but you may be carrying such a heavy weight of boredom, loneliness, doubt, pride, and/or hopelessness that you've forgotten how to unleash your creativity. The biblical perspective in this book will help you hear God's promptings more clearly and act on them with pure joy.

I encourage you to dream big dreams during this eye-opening, heart-pounding quest. Let me share with you forty proven, incremental steps that I personally have used for years and have coached my clients through—action steps that will help you to live a significance-filled life. God will be honored, and you will be blessed. You will find yourself empowered beyond your wildest imagination as you *Live Big!*

Will you take your first small step today?

PART 1
· · · · · · · · · · · ·
True Stories of Everyday Saints Living Big

TIP 1
....

Face Your Fears

Have you been caught in an unending stampede of fear about things that could go wrong in your life or in the lives of your loved ones? Are you looking for some relief from the worry that is consuming you? Do you even wonder if fear will prevent you from fulfilling an exhilarating, yet demanding, assignment from God? Do you wish there was a cure for your anxiety about all of this? Well, let me introduce you to Darlene, who by age forty had crowned herself the "Queen of Fear." She certainly learned a few things during her reign!

Darlene's countless fears were like a thick, sticky cobweb that entangled her at every step. Trepidation had such a stronghold on her that it frequently kept her immobile, unable to move forward. In desperation, she cried out to the Lord, writing to Him in her personal journal: "Who am I? What do You want to do with me during this stage of my life?" What happened during the next three years can only be attributed to God using

3

Darlene's circumstances to rescue her from her fears so she could focus on her purpose.

In January 2003, Darlene knew intuitively that she had to hop off life's speeding treadmill long enough to sit with God and hear from Him about the debilitating fear that was sabotaging His best plans for her life. Change was sorely needed. So, with God prompting her to take some downtime to regroup, she made the uncomfortable decision to leave her elementary-school teaching position, even though it had given her a great sense of security.

Fear and doubts ran rampant: *Why are you leaving what you love doing and are gifted to do? What are you going to do with yourself now? What about the salary loss?* She could barely breathe, but in obedience to God's leading, she stared down her fears by constantly reciting: "Trust in him at all times, you people; pour out your hearts to him, for God is our refuge" (Psalm 62:8).

Shortly after Darlene resigned from her job, her father died suddenly of a heart attack. Within two weeks, her mother's health declined rapidly as a result of Alzheimer's disease. Darlene ached with intense emotional pain day and night. Her parents had been married nearly fifty-two years. How could she even begin to process what had just happened and also be expected to clean out their entire home and disperse their belongings? Fear nearly squeezed her to death. She wondered: *Will this much stress cause me to have a heart attack, too? Am I destined to die suddenly like my dad, or will I slowly lose my mind like my mother? Which would be worse?*

Darlene took all of those foreboding fears to the Lord. She poured out her grief through tearful petitions and found enormous encouragement in this verse: "In this world you will have trouble. But take heart! I have overcome the world" (John 16:33).

As Darlene continued to look to God as her refuge, she began to sense His nudging her in September 2003 to expand her role as a mother, specifically through an international adoption of an older boy. The Lord had graciously allowed her to become a mother years earlier—after wrestling with infertility for many years—so this would be an added blessing.

The spin cycle of fear went into overdrive: *What if the boy doesn't bond with our family? How is he going to learn English? Will his personal story be so horrific that it causes him to "act out"? How much will the legal fees and overseas trips cost? Lord, do I even have what it takes to parent another preteen at my age?* God was persistent, though, and He kept showing Darlene and her husband, Phil, through His Word, prayer, Christian radio programs and magazine articles, and mature believers that He was on the move and that He wanted them to join Him.

Darlene and Phil embraced the adoption process. But on the same day they submitted their first large bundle of paperwork to the adoption agency, Darlene was informed that she needed a hysterectomy to remove a few small tumors. Her reaction: *Wow! Motherhood and a hysterectomy—all in the same breath. God must have a sense of humor in allowing those extreme circumstances to collide!*

The hysterectomy was scheduled. Darlene asked her family and prayer partners to join her in pouring out prayers, including praying for her fears about what might go wrong while under anesthesia and during the lengthy recovery time.

Within twenty-four hours after surgery, she knew that something had gone terribly wrong. Her lower abdomen was wracked with such severe pain that she drenched the bedsheets with sweat. Her fear escalated: *Am I going to die today?* She worried that the excruciating spasms would return at any moment, so she spent hours barely moving, taking only shallow breaths and thinking, *Why didn't the prayers work?*

She had expected to be out of the hospital three to four days after the surgery, so this complication had not been on her agenda. She was reminded, though, that God saw it all as she thought about the story in Genesis 16, in which Hagar was fearfully fleeing from Sarah's harsh treatment and found herself alone in the desert. Yet Hagar knew that God's watchful protection was on her even as she faced uncertainty. "[Hagar] gave this name to the LORD who spoke to her: 'You are the God who sees me'" (Genesis 16:13).

Tests revealed that Darlene's pain was from an accidental nick in her bladder during surgery that had left a dime-sized hole. Emergency surgery would be necessary. Her mind raced with fears: *What if the doctor goofs again? Do I have the strength to make it through a second surgery within seventy-two hours?* She laid these concerns before the Lord in prayer and submitted her life to Him once again. She knew that God was aware of her situation, but she really wanted to remind Him of the details! She was wheeled into surgery on Easter morning, the very day she was supposed to have been released—and all went well that Resurrection Day.

Life is full of twists and turns, but in the summer of 2005, God was orchestrating the long-delayed international adoption of a boy for Darlene and her family. They traveled to Ukraine to meet the nine-year-old, who was living in an orphanage. Traveling to a foreign country involves many unknowns, and Darlene had a suitcase full of fears. First were safety concerns—her family would be flying all night across the Atlantic Ocean; then a thirteen-hour train ride would take them deep into an unfamiliar land in the middle of the night to reach their destination at 5:30 A.M., in darkness. Then there were her fears about the language barrier, food differences, cultural nuances, and meeting the many demanding stipulations of an international adoption process, all while adjusting to the seven-hour time change. All of these worries kept Darlene pouring her heart out to God.

> [God] has a purpose in allowing bad things to happen, and his purpose extends not only to my life alone, but to the lives of others whom I may influence or help.
>
> Charles Stanley[1]

Darlene recalls arriving at their temporary apartment exhausted and full of apprehension. The anxiety really began to build when her family entered the dark, cold, gray lobby to take the tiny elevator up to the seventh floor. When the elevator door opened, they noticed a light bulb dangling precariously from a wire. They gingerly stepped inside, thinking of the likelihood of an electrical fire and that any substantial weight might plummet the dilapidated deathtrap downward. Darlene recounts the details of what happened next: "Instead of falling to our death as the elevator doors closed, an overwhelming odor of vomit gagged us. It was obvious from the stained walls that the smell had embedded itself into the concrete. We held our breath as long as we could, and I dared not focus on how many elevator rides we would be taking to and from our new flat during our stay."

The first adoption appointment proved challenging as seven people—Darlene and Phil, their two daughters, a translator, an administrator, and Igor, the young boy who was oh, so shy—packed into an undersized office. Later, after returning to their flat, Darlene was overcome with fear that Igor would not bond with her. She knew that bonding is the bedrock of any relationship, especially an adoption. While her husband took the girls to the market, she dropped to her knees in the apartment and cried out to God, begging Him to let her be able to look into the little boy's eyes during the next appointment and to let Igor see her unconditional love. In a heartfelt petition, Darlene asked the Lord for a miraculous breakthrough.

That evening, the family returned for another visit, and Igor excitedly met them with a small Bible that had a picture of Jesus with some children. Her future son began to share eagerly what was inside his special book, and he even occasionally made eye contact with a bashful smile. Her prayer had been answered. God definitely saw their situation and had His hand in this process. The long list of fears that nearly prevented Darlene from ever meeting her soon-to-be son had vanished into thin air!

Darlene was filled with new hope and confidence. Yet even her new-found courage did not prepare her for the coming tragedy.

In February 2006, her youngest brother died of cardiac arrest after his daily workout on the treadmill at his home. He was forty years old. As Darlene stood by his casket, she angrily told God that she felt as if He was playing a game of chess with her family as pawns. Fear that she might be the next to die screamed at her to stop being brave—and yet God miraculously used her brother's death to punctuate His desire to have Darlene cast her fears upon Him. Since God was still granting her breath, she chose to bow to His ways in obedience and give her fears to Him so she could carry a lighter load.

> Once you realize that you are able to learn new things and handle new situations, you cease fearing the future. People who have strong fears about the unknown have a strong need to "know everything" beforehand, and no one ever knows how to do something before they do it.
>
> Henry Cloud and
> John Townsend[2]

The juggling act of fear and faith had been so arduous through her infertility, career crisis, father's death, mom's Alzheimer's, tumors, surgeries, international adoption, and brother's death that, today, Darlene is adamant about not wasting any more time submitting to any more fears. God had stripped away her fears one by one, finally dethroning her as the "Queen of Fear." Now it was time to grow in His purpose and plan, and she could not have been more thrilled and grateful.

Darlene had followed God's advice and taken a tough step to slow down her life, which allowed her the opportunity to address each of her fears as it arose. In His kindness, God has blessed her family greatly, and now her joy overflows as she speaks to crowds at women's retreats and events. She still encounters fear (these days, it's a fear of writing as she creates handouts for studies that she teaches online and in person), but she claims boldly, "I'm workin' on it!"

Only God could have orchestrated this exciting time of her life. And in doing so, He has answered her two main questions: "Who am I?" and "What do You want to do with me during this stage of my life?" Darlene knows she is a beloved child of God and that she can trust Him in each and every season of her life to give her the perfect assignment.

What about you? Who are you? What does God want to do with you during this stage of your life?

Have you, like Darlene, been in situations that have taken you beyond your comfort zone and caused you to wonder how God can rescue you from the fears that haunt you? If so, pour out your heart to Him, naming your greatest fears and turning them over to Him. Don't fret; just take courage. Then you'll be able to say with Hagar that your faithful and almighty God is the God who sees you!

Five Action Steps from Your Life Coach

Fear can immobilize us and causes us great angst. It can even make us feel as if we're caught in a spin cycle of life—and desperately trying to get free. Do your fears include fear of failure, success, rejection, abandonment, being alone, or public humiliation? Whatever your worries might be, take one step today toward God and away from one of your fears. He wants to help you. He longs for you to live an abundant life, fulfilling the passionate purpose for which He created you. Here are five action steps for you to consider.

ACTION STEP 1: **Fast-forward your life by five years.** Daydream about what your life will look like with and without the fear. When you look ahead, what do you notice? Can you imagine the new fearless you?

ACTION STEP 2: **Pray for victory over fear.** Today's the day to decide whether you will be victorious over your fear or whether it will gain the victory over you. In prayer, take the matter before the Lord, and decide today whether you will live with fear or with courage.

Realize that nothing of value ever gets accomplished without prayer.

ACTION STEP 3: **Surrender a fear to your Maker.** Are you willing to let God take your fear now? Do something symbolic to surrender it. For example, you could write it on a stone and throw it into the ocean. Or you could write it on a piece of paper and bury it under a bush. Doing something physical can give you a visual and tactile reminder of your commitment.

ACTION STEP 4: **Check your fear dividends.** Each of our actions creates a dividend or payoff (e.g., sympathy, control, attention, extra help, or a "free pass" from contributing). Ask yourself, *What is the real payoff of my fear?* Knowing a partial motivator for your fear can speak volumes of truth into your life.

ACTION STEP 5: **Face the thief.** Fear keeps us focused on ourselves, and it robs us of many things, such as joy, creativity, adventure, freedom, productivity, opportunities, and/or relationships. Reclaim your stolen goods today by making a choice to seek the support you need in a small group or counseling setting.

REFLECTION

Think about how you would answer the following question as you read the rest of the book. We'll use your daydreaming about it in Tip 10: Capture Your *Live Big!* Dream. If you prefer to write your answer, you can jot it on a piece of paper or in a journal, or you can go to my ministry Web site, www.LifePurposeCoachingCenters.com, to download a great template to use for this exercise.

Basic premises

- If you had assurance from God that He was thrilled with your plans to follow your dream and that He would not let you fail . . .

- If you had all the time and energy you needed . . .

- If the entire world were eager to support your vision with money and resources . . .

- If this were the ideal season of your life . . .

Specific premise in this chapter

If you were free of all your fears . . . *what passionate,* Live Big! *dream would you pursue?*

Here's my answer to this reflection question, just in case it might help you remember to dream large:

If I were free of all my fears . . . I would buy a hundred acres of oceanfront property to open a Christian Life Coach Training Center, where I would oversee the training of staff for two hundred coaching centers worldwide. It would include personal living quarters for me and my guests (visiting grandkids!).

Prayer

Dear Lord, You will have to help me become fear-free, because I certainly can't do it alone. I know with all my heart that You want me to be strong and courageous. Send Your Holy Spirit to guide and strengthen me as Your Word promises: "The Spirit

God gave us does not make us timid, but gives us power, love and self-discipline" (2 Timothy 1:7). Because I know that fear keeps me focused on myself instead of on You, I choose freedom from fear today as I take one step toward fulfilling the destiny You desire for me. Amen.

Learn to Exhale

W E KNOW THAT BREATHING IN OXYGEN AND BREATHING out carbon dioxide is what keeps us alive. It is this vital work of our lungs that helps relax the body, calm the spirit, and clear the mind. God never intended for us to handicap ourselves with shallow breathing. That's no way to live life to the fullest! The breath of life is God's miraculous gift to us, both physically and spiritually. How fitting that the Greek word for *Holy Spirit* is *Pneuma* ($\pi\nu\varepsilon\acute{\upsilon}\mu\alpha$), which means "breath."

Did you know that remembering to exhale fully can be a particularly important skill for those who live with tension, worry, or unpredictability? Meet Kristi, who had to relearn the art of exhaling completely after a tough season of holding her breath and waiting for the other shoe to drop.

Kristi vividly recalls the moment she realized that she was exhaling only partially. She had just escaped an abusive marriage and was concerned about the emotional health of her six-year-old son—worried that the trauma of the divorce and unhealthiness of the aftermath might be negatively affecting him. She didn't want him to grow up angry or fearful, so she took him to see a therapist. After her son's first two appointments, Kristi was asked to come in for a private conference. *That's awesome!* she thought. *If it's already time for an update, they must be making great progress.*

The news was better than she could have hoped. The counselor said that Kristi's son appeared to be handling the divorce just fine, that he didn't seem to have any misplaced fear or anger, and that there would be no need for future visits. What a relief! She was so pleased. But the meeting did not end there. In fact, it was just getting started. The therapist went on to say that there was one glaring issue that her son had brought up during a session when asked to draw a picture of how he felt his mother was doing now that it was just the two of them.

Kristi stared at the sketch. She was aghast. It was a caricature of a woman with an abnormally huge head punctuated with large, bulging eyes and ears. It looked as if the head was going to explode. She couldn't even try to deny the resemblance, because her son had added her flowing blonde hair as well as lips that were perfectly outlined with the same plum color as the lipstick she always wore.

Is there any better wake-up call than a raw moment of truth from one's own child? This session certainly got Kristi's attention. She learned of her son's reply when the counselor had asked him if Mom seemed angry. The insightful youngster had said, "No, my mom's not angry, but she just looks like she's holding her breath and pretending that everything is fine. I never see her happy about anything we do."

As Kristi reflected on those remarks, she realized that she was living her life fearfully, expecting more drama to ensue, anticipating more turmoil. Subconsciously, she believed that if she could just hold her breath—or only allow herself to inhale and exhale extremely shallow breaths—she could fool herself into thinking that she was holding it all together and ensuring that nothing else in their fragile lives would fall apart. It was like living in an MRI machine, lying motionless, mouth closed, focusing on controlled nasal breathing—fearful of messing up the important images. Kristi's guarded behavior was creating a false sense of security and the illusion of control over the chaos.

But oxygen-infused breathing is part of our existence, and when we are not breathing deeply, we are not living fully. The emotional pressure of many years was bottled up inside Kristi, and by refusing to exhale completely, she had allowed the internal pressure to build to a dangerous level. And, frankly, that is where the enemy was thrilled to keep her.

> The thief comes only to steal and kill and destroy. I have come that they may have life, and have it to the full.
>
> John 10:10

Kristi's deer-in-the-headlights reaction to her circumstances was predictable for a woman who had grown up as a pastor's daughter. After all, church myth tells us that things like abuse aren't supposed to happen to faithful churchgoers, much less to a pastor's kid. She had spent much of her adult life worried about what the congregants would think if they found out that her marriage was not picture perfect. Now it was a moot point.

Because she had just been outed by her concerned little boy for not healing well, she decided she needed to take immediate action. Kristi joined a support group of women with their own stories of hurt, pain, and grief over the loss of a relationship. With the help of these new friends and her counselor, she eventually realized that the simple act of stopping for a moment to enjoy a good, long exhale was refreshing and freeing. It became the incredible sigh of life that told her she was still alive.

Kristi confesses: "I loved the process of learning to relax, although change didn't happen as easily as spontaneous combustion. Instead, it seemed to show up miraculously when I took one small step at a time." As she grew more confident about focusing forward, she asked God to identify the areas of growth that would most honor Him. He answered her, and she began to reject old patterns of emotional and spiritual abuse that occasionally crept back into her life. She also chose to guard against slipping back into her previous victim mentality, and so she strategically removed herself from unwholesome relationships and environments. And she finally realized that pretending everything was just fine had kept her too long from healing from the emotional wounds of the family pandemonium, so she admitted the hurt to those she could trust.

She found a picture of herself as a four-year-old playing

dress-up. That picture became a visual reminder of how Jesus saw her: beautiful, lovely, and full of joy. She put it in her wallet to keep uppermost in her mind that she is a precious daughter of the King, created to live every day in His presence, free from shame. That simple act helped Kristi reject berating comments that were based on unrealistic expectations. She reminded herself, *I am good enough in God's eyes!*

> Always be a first-rate version of yourself, instead of a second-rate version of somebody else.
>
> Judy Garland[1]

and grew daily to become more authentically herself instead of worrying about what others thought of her.

One day, as Kristi was practicing her breathing, she began to reflect on how Lamaze-patterned breathing had helped her years earlier to manage her pain during labor contractions. That specific breathing technique involves four rapid exhales ("hee, hee, hee, hee") to one blow ("hoo"). It had forced oxygen into Kristi's bloodstream, created a comfortable rhythm that relaxed her jaw and shoulders, and kept her focused on the task at hand. She knew that, although she didn't need to *hee-hoo* anymore, she definitely did need to keep exhaling on purpose, especially in difficult situations.

Kristi wondered if Queen Esther in the Bible had done any deep breathing during one of her most eventful and stressful incidents. Remember the story? Esther had an opportunity to save her people (the Jews) by appealing to the king, but because she had not been officially invited to speak with him, it meant she would be risking her life. If he declined to see her, the penalty for approaching the throne would be death. Kristi couldn't help but imagine Esther taking a deep breath and slowly exhaling several times before bravely answering her cousin's messenger, who had brought news of the plot to annihilate the Jewish people. Esther said, "Go, gather together all the Jews who are in Susa, and fast for me. Do not eat or drink for three days, night or day. I and my attendants will fast as you do. When this is done, I will go to the king, even though it is against the law. And if I perish, I perish" (Esther 4:16).

Kristi often meditated on that passage in order to remain strong whenever her courage wavered. She learned to obey God's nudges peacefully instead of operating out of fear of man or woman. She found herself experiencing new joys each day, learning to trust the God who first exhaled and breathed life into Adam and generations to come. She was more ready now to accept that God had created her in His own image, and she delighted like a child in finding her identity in Christ. She grew in her understanding of what living with godly character looks like, as the apostle Paul described it: "The fruit of the Spirit is love, joy, peace, patience, kindness, goodness, faithfulness, gentleness and self-control" (Galatians 5:22–23).

> Women give birth to ideas, to creative expressions, to ministries. We birth life in others by inviting them into deeper realms of healing, to deeper walks with God, to deeper intimacy with Jesus.
> John and Stasi Eldredge[2]

Finally, Kristi felt free to live her life to the fullest. As she entered this new season, she sensed that God had a distinct plan for her in addition to her sacred trust of being a mom. Much like the physical birth of her son years earlier, she now believed that it was time to give birth to an additional, amazing life purpose that God had planted deep in her soul—a dream for which she had been magnificently created. She fervently wanted to live out her God-breathed giftedness and talents in a way that would help other women heal from their hurts and experience the joy and freedom that come from breathing deeply. Today she helps them take steps toward giving birth to their own dreams.

Kristi's son has now graduated from college. He lives with a joy and inner peace that can only come from God. He has a heart for those less fortunate, and he is an inspiration to his mom and others. Kristi is now married to a wonderful, God-sent man, and she lives in daily

> He who began a good work in you will carry it on to completion until the day of Christ Jesus.
>
> Philippians 1:6

gratitude for that tremendous blessing. She laughs as she says, "At our wedding reception, I made sure we took an all-important picture of me smiling to show off my plum lipstick and average-sized, nonexploding head!" She has begun a new and exciting chapter of her life, confident in God's personalized plan for her.

What about you? Does breathing deeply sound to you like a

much-needed relief right now? Is it time for you to get a new lease on an attractive life? Are you ready to stop fretting and start living the abundant life?

Five Action Steps from Your Life Coach

Shallow breathing makes for shallow living. It shortcuts all of the goodness in God's plan, which is extravagant, abundant, broad-reaching, and life-giving. It robs us of our chance to "soar on wings like eagles" (Isaiah 40:31). A slow, deep inhale-exhale makes all the difference to us physically and emotionally. Try it right now, several times.

Feeling better already? Here are five action steps for you to implement as you learn to exhale.

ACTION STEP 1: **Retreat annually.** Take some time each year to get away by yourself, breathe, and reassess who and what are important in your life. Come home feeling refreshed and able to take definitive steps.

ACTION STEP 2: **Cultivate deep friendships.** Seek out the friendship of other women who will walk with you in the tough times and encourage you as you grow in your faith and learn to exhale. Go on a friend search today!

ACTION STEP 3: **Schedule fun.** To start intentionally

living with more joy, happiness, and fun in your life, actually schedule blocks of time in your calendar, and give yourself permission to relax and spend more time with family and friends. Keep marking these on your calendar—and sticking to them—until they become a natural part of your newly balanced life.

ACTION STEP 4: **Select key scriptures.** Write three of your favorite Bible verses about God's love for you on index cards, and put them in your purse or backpack. Read them on a daily basis until you actually start to believe God's truth about who you are in Christ and that He has a plan for your life.

ACTION STEP 5: **Let humor help.** Look for the humor in everyday situations instead of getting frustrated and tense when things don't go the way you intend. Remember that laughing is a healthy way of releasing bottled-up tension. Think of it as extra-strength breathing therapy!

REFLECTION

Think about the following question as you read the rest of the book. We'll use your daydreaming about it in Tip 10: Capture Your *Live Big!* Dream.

Basic premises

- If you had assurance from God that He was thrilled with your plans to follow your dream and that He would not let you fail . . .

- If you had all the time and energy you needed . . .

- If the entire world were eager to support your vision with money and resources . . .

- If this were the ideal season of your life . . .

Specific premises in the two chapters so far

1. If you were free of all your fears . . .

2. If you truly had discovered the benefits and joy of exhaling . . . *what passionate*, Live Big! *dream would you pursue?*

I'm excited about my answer to this reflection question:

If I truly had discovered the benefits and joy of exhaling . . . I would take ballroom dance lessons.

Prayer

Heavenly Father, You breathed life into Adam and into me, too. Thank You. As I learn to rest in Your love each day, I pray that Your Holy Spirit would continue to breathe new life into me and those around me. Teach me to inhale Your grace and truth—and to exhale all that is keeping me from Your best. Thank You for the joy I experience as I relax into the beauty of the purposes for which You undeniably created me. Thank You for Your faithfulness. Amen.

Honor Your Deepest Longings

W E CAN LIVE THE LIFE WE IMAGINE! IN FACT, WE CAN DO more than we ever imagined. And few things are as gratifying as the success of making a dream come true and having accomplished the seemingly impossible. Would you like to wipe a few "what ifs" from the whiteboard of your life? Are you willing to step out of your comfort zone today and experience the thrill of taking a risk by honoring the dream that has long been inside you?

Judy decided that it was time to live her dream. Her first child, Sara, was college-bound at last. The big send-off day had finally arrived, and it was filled with exhilarating and exhausting activity—tromping up and down the dormitory stairs a dozen times, running the obstacle course over and around boxes in the hallway, the hustle and bustle of lunch in the

> I have learned, that if one advances confidently in the direction of his dreams, and endeavors to live the life he has imagined, he will meet with a success unexpected in common hours.
>
> Henry David Thoreau.[1]

cafeteria, parent orientation, and meeting the roommate.

At day's end, Sara stood in the university's courtyard waving good-bye to Mom and Dad while they walked to their car, leaving their firstborn to face the next few weeks on her own. As Judy and her husband, Mark, drove away from the college campus that day, Judy was a train wreck of emotions. A million thoughts swirled through her mind: *Will Sara be OK? Will she make friends? Will she come home on weekends? Will she still need me?* Along with these maternal questions came the typical self-reflection inquiry: *What will I do now?* And then, one random thought came out of nowhere: *In a few years, I will be the only member of this family without a college degree.*

Judy allowed her mind to wander back to the years before marriage and children, when medical school was her constant and fervent desire. To be a doctor, that's all she had ever wanted in a career; it's what she had craved. She remembered being tantalizingly close to choosing medicine but walking away from it to pursue her other passion: marriage and family. She had to let go of one dream to realize another fully.

Because it would be a long drive home from the college campus, Judy chose temporarily to shake off the sadness that always hovered just below the surface in her life. She wiped her tears and bravely tried to suppress her feelings. Throughout the next few months, however, thoughts of her own college education were constantly sneaking up on her. She took a firm stance against those intruders: *I'm too old. It will take too long. I can't afford it. My family will think I'm crazy. Younger students will laugh at me. I don't have the time.* Day after day, feelings bubbled up inside her as if she were wrestling with God, just as Jacob had (Genesis 32:24–30). Her angst was so intense that it was almost a physical pain. Finally, lifting her hands toward heaven, she cried out to God, as did Jacob: "I will not let you go unless you bless me" (Genesis 32:26).

Slowly, over the next six months, while cradling the idea as gingerly as if it were a glass ornament that would surely break, Judy allowed the potentiality of living out her dream to settle in and come to rest in the depths of her soul: *What if I were able to get a school loan? What if there were online courses? What if I could find a school that will take my previous college credits? What if I actually graduated?* But then the dismissal would always follow: *No, that's silly. I've missed my window of opportunity.*

One night, she inaudibly perceived this rebuttal to her argument: *No, you haven't. You're just afraid.*

Wait, she thought. *That wasn't me saying that.*

Then she thought she heard: *No, it's Me.*

She dared to inquire: *God?*

And she sensed His reply: *Yes.*

That's ridiculous! Judy countered. *I'm not afraid. I loved school.* Instantly, she heard the truth in her heart: *You are afraid.*

You're afraid of failing. You're afraid of not finishing. You're afraid of your children finishing before you. You're afraid of letting the dream live again.

Judy sat on her patio in the dark that night for a long time. At the top of her prayer journal page, she scrawled: "Am I really afraid? Can I really do this?"

Then God began to remind Judy of Scripture passages. They came flooding into her mind so quickly that it was hard to scribble the words fast enough:

- "I can do all this through him who gives me strength" (Philippians 4:13).
- "The LORD is trustworthy in all he promises and faithful in all he does" (Psalm 145:13).
- "The one who calls you is faithful, and he will do it" (1 Thessalonians 5:24).

God's loving promises soon filled a dozen pages of Judy's notebook. She wept as the dream she had buried began to fight its way through the years of darkness and doubt. The longing she thought had died long ago was now humbly reborn, leaving her speechless and in absolute awe of God.

In no time at all, the pieces of the "I'm actually going to do this" puzzle fell into place so easily that Judy was confident the road map was God's best for her life. She had clear answers to the questions of where, when, and how to complete her bachelor's degree. Her family, having been privy to her initial daunting fears, became a source of constant encouragement and advice. This was no longer a someday wish; it was a God-inspired, joy-filled mission being cheered on by a slew of enthusiastic supporters. And remarkably, not once during the long nights of cranking out papers and cramming for exams did she ever think of quitting.

At last, with the final assignment submitted, Judy thought back to that night on the porch when God let the hope rise within her. In overwhelming gratitude, she whispered aloud, "God, thank You for not giving up on Your/my dream!"

Soon this mother of grown children was holding the college diploma that conferred upon her, Judith Arlene Grandstrand, a bachelor of science degree in Christian education. She let the enormity of the achievement sink in, and then she heard herself loudly exclaim, "I did it! I actually did it!" At the graduation party, Sara gave her a Barbie doll dressed as the Scarecrow character in *The Wizard of Oz,* who pursued his dream of getting a brain. That doll is now a prized possession, a fun symbol of a mission accomplished.

Fast-forward ten years . . .

Our gracious God took Judy's initial dream of becoming a doctor and healing the physically ill, and He enlarged her vision to include healing those who are suffering mentally and emotionally. In hot pursuit of that goal, Judy has completed two bachelor's degrees, a master's in counseling, and training in lay ministry and chaplaincy. Now she has added the letters NHD (Natural Health Doctor) after her name, fulfilling her dream of helping people with nutrition, stress reduction, and disease prevention.

Today, Judy and Mark dare to dream about serving in Africa, and their united cry has become *Lord, we will go where You want us to go.* In preparation for what might be, the couple recently spent three weeks traveling across South Africa to get a feel for the land and the people, falling in love with both. As this opportunity begins to unfold, they wait patiently for God's timing, listening for His confirming voice. Together they pray these prayers:

- "Speak, for your servants are listening" (adapted from 1 Samuel 3:10).
- "Stand at the crossroads and look . . . ask where the good way is, and walk in it, and you will find rest for your souls" (Jeremiah 6:16).

Judy's life is so much richer now than she ever imagined it could be. She humbly declares, "Joy springs up daily from my heart that is full." Has God given you a passionate ache that you've hidden away? Is there a stirring in your soul that you dare to think about but not act upon?

- What if you truly understood that our God is not a God of small, inconsequential dreams?
- What if you redefined success as the willingness to accept God's call on your life, to pursue His dream for you creatively?
- What if you really believed that, with God, there is no room for doubt?
- What if you learned to trust Him in and for all things?

- What if you decided to fulfill your dream in spite of the risks involved?

Rejoice that it is possible to take one step today toward honoring your longings and having all of your dreams come true!

Five Action Steps from Your Life Coach

Some people think they don't have time to dream. I say we don't have time *not* to dream!

> Twenty years from now you will be more disappointed by the things that you didn't do than by the ones you did do. So throw off the bowlines. Sail away from the safe harbor. Catch the trade winds in your sails. Explore. Dream. Discover.
>
> Mark Twain[2]

Dreaming leads us to say no to other people's agendas for us. It cuts down on the waste and nonsense in our lives because it allows us to stay focused on what's really important to us. It teaches us to stop filling our time with activities that numb us into a false sense of happiness or with things that cause us to stuff down our feelings of hopelessness. God created you to live out His dream for your life, not to spend all of your time in the doldrums that weigh you down. So here are five steps that will help you live in freedom as you honor your deepest longings.

ACTION STEP 1: **Check in with God.** If a dream of making a contribution won't die, there's a good chance it's a God-commissioned and anointed dream. Get alone with the Master Planner for several hours, and ask Him!

ACTION STEP 2: **Give the dream back to God.**
A dream, when surrendered to God, becomes much
bigger than we can ever imagine on our own. Give it
completely to Him, and be willing to follow where He
leads.

ACTION STEP 3: **Trust God, the giver of dreams.** God
is ever faithful and true. He will never let you down.
He will be there with you, supplying your every need:
time, energy, resources, network, platform, courage, creativity, and much more. Trust Him as the Great Provider.

ACTION STEP 4: **Adapt the best practices of those
with a similar dream.** Keep your eyes open for things
that will save you from having to reinvent the wheel.
Adapt the best practices of people and organizations
with sterling track records. Whenever possible, ask others about their successes and failures. Be honest with
them that you are attempting to reduce your learning
curve.

ACTION STEP 5: **Keep moving forward!** Create an
initial to-do list of what it will take to make your specific
longing a reality. Then enlist others to help you create
a time line, and work on the list with you. Remember,
if the dream is from God, you won't be able to do it by

yourself anyway. In fact, God often prefers to send an army of supporters to get His jobs done. Even if you can't see the entire picture yet, move forward with confidence, keeping your eyes on the God of all wisdom and on the horizon.

REFLECTION

Think about the following question as you read the rest of the book. We'll use your daydreaming about it in Tip 10: Capture Your *Live Big!* Dream.

Basic premises

- If you had assurance from God that He was thrilled with your plans to follow your dream and that He would not let you fail . . .

- If you had all the time and energy you needed . . .

- If the entire world were eager to support your vision with money and resources . . .

- If this were the ideal season of your life . . .

Specific premises in the three chapters so far

1. If you were free of all your fears . . .

2. If you truly had discovered the benefits and joy of exhaling . . .

3. If you honored your deepest longings . . . *what passionate*, Live Big! *dream would you pursue?*

This reflection question stirred up a lot of emotion for me. It may for you as well.

If I honored my deepest longings . . . I would convert my "life's work" of twenty Life Purpose Coach E-Workbook training guides into a published training manual to be sold in bookstores, and I would hire a top-notch screenwriter to make a movie about a woman's search for purpose.

Prayer

God, I thank You for giving me a dream, even though it can get somewhat buried at times. Thank You for being faithful to Your Word, which says, "Trust in the Lord with all your heart and lean not on your own understanding; in all your ways submit to him, and he will make your paths straight" (Proverbs 3:5–6). Give me the courage to step out in faith and trust You to direct me down the pathway toward my God-size dreams. You have always been there for me. I know how deeply You love me. And, like Jacob, I am fully expecting a blessing that will have an impact on generations to come. Above all else, though, I want to say that I will love You forever—over and above the dream! You are worthy to be praised for who You are rather than for how You bless me. Amen.

Don't Ever Give Up

MAKING A ONCE-AND-FOR-ALL-TIME DECISION TO BE A woman of perseverance is one of the most important and life-changing things you could ever do. If you and others know that you are not going to quit, not going to give up, not going to stop short of the finish line, you and they will have a confidence in you that is priceless. Being a woman who keeps her commitments to people and projects is not only refreshing in our microwave, throw-away society, but it also is a huge part of God's plan for you as you complete the mission He has set before you. Enjoy Jamie's story of perseverance, which is an encouragement to those of us who often feel like giving up.

Jamie's lessons about perseverance started at age thirteen in Nova Scotia, Canada, while she was on vacation with her family. Entering a restaurant, she heard the screech of tires outside and turned in time to see a car slamming into a motorcycle, with the driver of the bike tumbling end-over-end. She ran toward the victim and found him unconscious. A bystander shouted at her to call an ambulance, but when the telephone operator asked for the location of the crash and cursory details of the victim's injuries, Jamie realized that she didn't even know the name of the town, let alone any other particulars.

The panic she experienced that day stayed with her throughout the rest of the trip, and Jamie decided that she would never allow herself to be so helpless again in a life-or-death situation. In fact, this young girl made a gutsy decision that day to become an emergency medical technician (EMT) as soon as she was old enough.

Back home, Jamie immediately set to work earning a Girl Scout first-aid badge. She packed an emergency bag for her family to keep in their car and studiously took notes on every episode of *Emergency!*—a popular television show about paramedics. It became common to see makeshift splints and eye patches on neighborhood dogs and cats who were willing subjects for her practice sessions. Jamie's determination to follow through on her conviction was evident to all.

When she was eighteen, a listing for an EMT class in a local university catalog jumped off the page and gripped her heart; she knew it was time to formalize her training. As the youngest student and one of the few females in the class, Jamie constantly challenged herself with taxing extra-credit assignments. At that time, it was considered appropriate for women to work at a medical office or hospital, but it was nearly unthinkable that they would have the physical and emotional ability to handle trauma in the woods or on the streets. Even with her behemoth effort, it was difficult to press through her classmates' preconceived notion of her supposed lack of abilities. Jamie knew that was unfair, but she simply made up her mind to do everything with 200-percent effort and stamina. She persevered even though the odds were stacked against her, and she was proud to receive her EMT certification one glorious summer day.

> Never give in, never give in, *never, never, never*—in nothing, great or small, large or petty—never give in except to convictions of honour and good sense.
>
> Winston Churchill[1]

Soon after, Jamie became a wilderness search-and-rescue volunteer, trudging for days through mosquito-infested cedar swamps to look for lost hunters and snowmobiling through howling blizzards to rescue stranded motorists. Jamie recalls, "I am not an outdoorsy person by nature. I have never been much of a camper, and I hate bugs. To say that I value indoor plumbing is an understatement! But being on that squad meant greater exposure to more rescue situations, and I needed the experience in the worst way, despite the high price it cost me emotionally and physically."

She knew that the men of the squad, though not unkind, thought of her as a "token" female. But all of that changed one day during a flood. As a result of melting snow and subsequent pouring rain, a river that ran through a town had overflowed its banks, cutting off an entire neighborhood. Jamie and her partner were sent to evacuate those residents. Her partner drove their brand-new rescue truck slowly through the high waters, being careful not to dislodge the boat they were towing. Suddenly, their vehicle got caught in the raging river, veered off the road, and quickly began to submerge. As the water rose above the dashboard, Jamie's thoughts went from *Interesting predicament* to *God, save us!* She squeezed through an open window to grab a rope and anchor from the boat so she could tie the truck to a log guardrail, preventing further damage to the vehicle. Her quick thinking was praised, and she was happy to find that, afterward, the reservations of her teammates seemed to vanish.

After several years in search and rescue, Jamie applied to be a member of the sheriff department's R-52 team, an elite specialist unit that saved drowning victims, stranded mountain climbers, and injured survivors trapped in auto wreckage. Well-meaning friends advised her against trying for the position because they believed she would not have the upper-body strength to qualify. Besides, no other woman had ever worked in this service, and the application process was notoriously rigorous.

> Most of the important things in the world have been accomplished by people who have kept on trying when there seemed to be no help at all.
>
> Dale Carnegie[2]

Regardless, Jamie persevered in her efforts, believing that this was a large part of her destiny. She interviewed well but then was terrified to be accepted. She knew that excellence was a basic job requirement, not an optional, nice-to-have quality. Her ability to perform and persist through impossible situations would be pivotal, as an example not only to other women who would someday follow in her footsteps but, more important, to those she would be attempting to rescue.

Part of Jamie's training was spent in an auto salvage yard learning to operate the Jaws of Life—a sixty-five-pound hydraulic, car-dismantling tool that is not only heavy but unwieldy. On the first day, weighed down by bulky firefighting gear and peering through the plastic shield of her face piece, Jamie hefted the tip of the Jaws to the door hinge she was assigned to break. The twelve men of the unit gathered in a semicircle around her to watch. Some jeered, but soon she could hear nothing beyond the roar of blood in her ears. Slowly, the metal on the car door stretched, and little by little, one hinge gave way as she shifted the rescue device to a better position. She dared not look around at the men standing nearby with their arms folded.

Her own arms shook, and her knees trembled as the weight became too much to hold. As if on cue, the memory of the man tumbling off his motorcycle flashed through Jamie's mind, a reminder of the stomach-knotting panic and fear she had felt as a young girl. Tightening her grip and gritting her teeth, a grunt escaped from somewhere deep in her belly. Then, amazingly, the door gave way and popped off its hinges. Trying to appear nonchalant, she casually lowered the Jaws to the ground and stepped back as though completing this assignment were an everyday occurrence. The guys, their eyebrows raised, nodded and went back to their training. She stood, body trembling from exertion, heart pounding, and sweat pouring down her back. She remembers desperately wanting to raise her hands in the air and shout, "Yes!" Instead, she smiled and quietly asked, "Is there anything else?"

Jamie laughs as she retells the sequel to that story: "The next day, I woke up and couldn't raise my arms, even to put on a blouse. To brush my teeth, I had to rest my elbow on my bathroom vanity and rotate my head side-to-side! Catching a glimpse of my silly, sideways grin in the mirror, I took a moment to congratulate myself for having stick-to-it-iveness with a goal that was so important to me."

> Consider it pure joy, my brothers and sisters, whenever you face trials of many kinds, because you know that the testing of your faith produces perseverance. Let perseverance finish its work so that you may be mature and complete, not lacking anything.
>
> James 1:2–4

Certification took years to earn, and Jamie was ready to quit many times (especially during ice-rescue training). Each time, though, she resolved anew to persevere until the job was complete.

The Bible is loaded with stories about ordinary men and women who experienced great adversity and unrelenting pressure yet found their character growing immensely when they decided to stay the course. Simon Peter, for example, left his fishing boats behind and began walking dusty paths with other imperfect disciples. He spent three years on a steep learning curve, being pummeled with hardships as a disciple of Jesus, but he did not give up trying to be a loving and faithful follower. He faced hostile crowds, had countless moments of weakness, was frequently puzzled by Jesus's parables, and struggled with a brash, outspoken demeanor and impulsive bravado. But he kept trying.

And finally, one glorious day, he was able to give a dramatic declaration of faith (Matthew 16:16), which prompted Jesus to reply: "Blessed are you, Simon son of Jonah, for this was not revealed to you by flesh and blood, but by my Father in heaven. And I tell you that you are Peter, and on this rock I will build my church, and the gates of death will not overcome it. I will give you the keys of the kingdom of heaven" (Matthew 16:17–19).

Yet Peter still stumbled through a series of fateful incidents the night before Jesus was crucified. First, Peter fell asleep in the Garden of Gethsemane instead of staying awake to pray; then he denied knowing his best friend, Jesus, three times (Matthew 26:69–75). When we read that Peter wept bitterly over his unfaithfulness, it's easy to imagine his shame and his urge to quit and go back to his nets and the sea. Though Peter would have had every reason to give up, he instead chose to begin anew, persevering to complete the purpose for which he had been created and commissioned. In fact, his strong leader-

> We also glory in our sufferings, because we know that suffering produces perseverance; perseverance, character; and character, hope. And hope does not put us to shame, because God's love has been poured out into our hearts through the Holy Spirit, who has been given to us.
>
> Romans 5:3–5

ship of the early church provided stability and fostered growth, and his vision in Acts 11 changed the course of the church forever.

Today, each of us has the opportunity to decide whether we will persevere in a certain area of our life. The earthly rewards are immeasurable when we do so; they include a deep sense of significance and joy. And the heavenly rewards are beyond our ability to comprehend. But to live out our purpose requires single-minded focus, dedication, discipline, and perseverance. There's little room for quitters!

Five Action Steps from Your Life Coach

Persevering always comes at a price. Sometimes the cost is time and resources, but other times the currency is loss of comfort, control, or perhaps even a friendship. As Jamie found out, making the decision to pursue her goal was only the beginning. It was her action steps that took her greatest resolve, especially in the face of naysayers. In which area of your life is God asking you to persevere? In your marriage, family, career, ministry, finances, education, exercise plan, sobriety? How about the resilience needed in discovering and fulfilling God's matchless call on your life? Whatever it is, these action steps will help you go the distance.

ACTION STEP 1: **Check your motives.** Assess your long-term commitment by taking a few prayerful moments to lay your desires and motives before the Lord. Knowing more about the reasons or motives for your goal will help you persevere.

ACTION STEP 2: **Find an Aaron.** Surround yourself with friends who can speak the truth to you yet are unwaveringly supportive and encouraging. They can help prop up your arms when you're exhausted, as Aaron did for Moses, or they can give you the stern "Get up and get moving" talk that is sometimes needed.

ACTION STEP 3: **Practice staying power.** In order to ensure that you will complete the more difficult tasks in life, practice by persevering in something less dramatic, such as paying bills on time, attending church services, tithing, or eating healthy meals.

ACTION STEP 4: **Give up the "instant replay" in your mind.** Stop the endless ruminations of the "shoulda, woulda, coulda" cycle of regret. Focus forward, not in your rearview mirror!

ACTION STEP 5: **Try something new.** It's important to focus on your goal, but it's also important to take the time occasionally to do something completely unexpected, spontaneous, or outrageously different. The change will shake things up, and the invigorating infusion of fresh perspective will give you the energy you need to keep going. Try it!

REFLECTION

Think about the following question as you read the rest of the book. We'll use your daydreaming about it in Tip 10: Capture Your *Live Big!* Dream.

Basic premises

- If you had assurance from God that He was thrilled with your plans to follow your dream and that He would not let you fail . . .

- If you had all the time and energy you needed . . .

- If the entire world were eager to support your vision with money and resources . . .

- If this were the ideal season of your life . . .

Specific premises in the four chapters so far

1. If you were free of all your fears . . .

2. If you truly had discovered the benefits and joy of exhaling . . .

3. If you honored your deepest longings . . .

4. If you knew for sure that you would persevere to the end of the race . . . *what passionate, Live Big!* *dream would you pursue?*

My answer to this reflection question makes me smile. I hope yours affects you the same way!

If I knew for sure that I would persevere to the end of the race . . . I would update our ministry's business and marketing plans and then proceed, in faith, with having architectural renderings made of our many proposed buildings.

Prayer

Lord, like a child waiting for the first day of summer vacation, I am beyond excited to see what You have in store for me if I persevere to the end of what I know to do. You are the author of big dreams, and I wait with hopeful anticipation to see more clearly where You are leading. I pray that I will not waiver, falter, or doubt Your direction. Regardless of the results of our adventure, though, keep my eyes on the priority of getting to know You better during the journey and on my heavenly reward of seeing You face-to-face. Amen.

Use Your Past for Good

WHEN WE DEAL HONESTLY WITH OUR PAST AND SEE IT AS A ministry-influencing opportunity, we receive an extra portion of hope. Healing from the wounds in our past helps put our future into godly perspective, because we then understand that our heavenly Father has seen everything we've gone through, and we realize that He desires to use it all for Kingdom-building purposes. That frees us to live an authentic, truthful life rather than a life of pretense and secrecy, in which we attempt to hide from the ghosts of our past.

Are you doing the hard work of healing? Are you willing to face your past, to put it in the hands of our Lord and press forward? Natasha is a woman who has braved the agony of defeat on many fronts, and she is a firsthand witness to how God can use such experiences to bring good out of bad. Here's her story.

Natasha grew up in a loving Christian family in South Africa. She did well in school and was an overachiever in sports. She had dreams of becoming an Olympic star and looked forward to a bright future. Little did she know that her life was not going to follow the idyllic course she had outlined.

When Natasha was finishing high school, her father died in a tragic car accident. It was a pivotal year for her as she dealt with a broken heart and the unrelenting question, *Why did my dad have to die?* She plummeted into a depression that led to a suicide attempt and hospitalization. It was then that she became entangled by mistaken thinking about her lack of value in God's eyes.

As she began to process the loss of her dad a little more rationally, she overheard a relative's cutting remark: "Natasha will never amount to anything." Natasha embarked on a lifelong quest to prove that statement false. She sought self-worth by taking charge. She got a job, worked hard, and went to school part-time, taking courses in tourism and public relations. In her mid-twenties she met her husband, got pregnant, and then got married. In terms of a secular lifestyle, she had everything most women could only dream of having.

But she remembers waking up in the mornings with tears running down her cheeks and feeling guilty for not being happy. She always had a gut-level feeling that God had a unique role for her but that she was not in sync or living up to her full potential. Natasha hungered for what all people want: a sense of fulfillment. She hid her fear that she wouldn't measure up by trying to be the perfect wife, mom, and friend. But soon after the birth of her second child, a chain of horrible events spun her life out of control.

Her husband had several affairs, and his guilt triggered a crushing nightmare of physical and emotional abuse for Natasha. Eventually, he left her for another woman. He declared bankruptcy, and Natasha lost everything she owned in one day: her house, furniture, cars, everything. Soon after, she noticed that she was also losing most of her married-women friends. This is common among divorcees, but it shook Natasha to her core. She also had to deal with the discovery that her husband had been charged with fraud. Her family tried to be supportive, but they had their own hectic lives to lead. She felt very alone.

Natasha tried to cope with the heartache of deception and loss while trying to feed two hungry babies and not knowing where she would get money to survive. In a desperate attempt to put food on the table and a roof over their heads, she had an affair with a married man who provided for her and her children. Feelings of guilt led her into drugs, and she hit rock bottom, stripped of all self-worth once again.

Natasha got lost in her past and gave up hope of finding her way back. But there are no hopeless people in God's eyes. Not Natasha; not Mary Magdalene, a woman from whom Jesus cast out seven demons (Luke 8:1–3). Natasha recalls getting up one morning, having cried all night, too ashamed to pray, when God spoke to her through a particular Bible passage: " 'I know the plans I have for you,' declares the LORD, 'plans to prosper you and not to harm you, plans to give you hope and a future. Then you will call on me and come and pray to me, and I will listen to you. You will seek me and find me when you seek me with all your heart'" (Jeremiah 29:11–13).

She realized that, with all of the sadness she had felt, she had been focusing on her pain and problems instead of on God's power and love for her. She was now desperate enough to find her faith in Jesus alone.

> Sometimes He allows us to suffer so that we become a display case for His glory.
>
> Anne Graham Lotz[1]

Natasha knew that God never wastes a hurt and that He could be glorified through all of her circumstances. She knew that He wanted to use her pain to prepare her heart, mind, body, and soul to receive and worship Him. Sensing a flicker of light in the darkness, she started allowing Him to pick up the pieces of her battered life. It would take a miracle for her to overcome her feelings of worthlessness, but God was ever so patient and guided her slowly and lovingly through the small steps she needed to take.

An amazing spiritual journey ensued. Natasha began to converse with God all day long. She got into the habit of memorizing Scripture, convinced that this was essential in maintaining a great relationship with her Maker. She kept a spiritual journal in which she praised God for everything He had done for her. She also started humbly practicing the spiritual habits of repentance and fasting, and she began to feel at peace, cherishing the beautiful relationship God was allowing her to have with Him. She came across this quote by Judith Couchman which sums up her spiritual journey: "God specializes in taking the 'weaklings' of the world and turning them into strong and beautiful souls. In his eyes brokenness is not a failure; it is the gateway to a deeper spirituality."[2]

Several years later, Natasha fell in love with and married Fred Swanepoel, who became her pillar, cheering her on to be all God wants her to be. She glows as she says, "Fred's deep love and inspirational kindness are a true example of Christ's love." The couple got involved in their local church, and Natasha found joy in serving on the Intercessory Prayer Team and Women's Ministry Team. She and her cell group made it a habit to visit the elderly and children who needed encouragement and prayer.

God began using all of that effort to mold Natasha's character with traits such as patience, mercy, and perseverance. She was learning to be content with her daily purposes and to fulfill her day-to-day roles with great joy. She surrendered her past (including her father's death; her depression and suicide attempt; her ex-husband's adultery, abuse, bankruptcy, and fraud; her shame, affair, and addiction) and her relationship with her children and with Fred to the Lord for His use.

> Forgetting what is behind and straining toward what is ahead, I press on toward the goal to win the prize for which God has called me heavenward in Christ Jesus.
>
> Philippians 3:13–14

With a devoted support structure in place and with a return to normalcy and a family routine, Natasha found herself dreaming again of what she wanted to do with her life. But because of her immense gratitude that an ordinary woman from a Third World country could find a fairy-tale ending, her daydreams automatically centered around what she wanted to be and do for God. Then, miraculously, she found herself upgrading her prayers to ask God to reveal what *He* preferred to do in and through her.

Natasha's multiple crises and her passion for the Lord gave her a deep desire to walk alongside other women as they discover all God created them to be. She is particularly drawn to those who are broken and authentic, those who have experienced hardship and are ready to lead surrendered lives. A career in psychology seemed like a natural sequel to Natasha's life experiences, so she completed a BA in psychology—only to realize that God had different plans for her upon graduation. She followed His prompting and traveled to the United States for a short stay to become certified in Christian coaching. She now had confirmation that no hurt happened in vain and that God wanted to use her past for good. She considers it the greatest privilege she could ever imagine to chat with women about the kindness of God and the phenomenon of restora-

> We know that in all things God works for the good of those who love him, who have been called according to his purpose.
> Romans 8:28

tion. She tells everyone, "I have been blessed beyond measure!"

Natasha's dream now is to become a motivational speaker so she can share what God has done for her. She will open the first coaching center in South Africa and travel to various African countries, offering workshops and retreat camps for those less fortunate.

So, in regard to your own life, please know that no matter how broken or alone you feel, God is willing to weave every thread of your past into His Kingdom tapestry. He doesn't run from our hurts or failures; He restores us with grace and second chances. He is present with you this very moment, asking you to prepare yourself to follow His lead and do His work. Are you willing to let God use your past for good? If so, the only remaining question is, what would your most excellent dream look like?

Five Action Steps from Your Life Coach

It can make you feel uncomfortable and embarrassed if you think people only associate you with your past and don't see you for who you have grown up to be. But let's face it, sometimes you are the only person dredging up your past! You may have had relatively little grief in your life, or you may have endured terrible sorrow, but God has chosen to use every aspect of your story in His plan. He wants to use your past, whatever it is, for His good. Here are five steps that will help you do just that.

ACTION STEP 1: **Grab the good!** Don't miss out on the small joys of life by focusing on your past. Relish the opportunities that come your way today. Think of one fun way you could celebrate your next success or victory. (Recommendation: Find a way to celebrate that isn't based on sugar or caffeine!)

ACTION STEP 2: **Team up with Christian role models.** We all know the power of hanging out with positive role models. Their inspiration rubs off on us. Let a godly person be a powerful influence in your life. Contact someone this week to set up an appointment to chat about how God has used his or her past for good. (Important note from your wise Life Coach: If you are a married woman meeting with a man or an unmarried woman meeting with a married man, take someone with you.)

ACTION STEP 3: **Write and share your testimony.** Write about what has happened in your life. Showcase God's grace and how He healed you. Share your insights with someone about God's use of your past.

ACTION STEP 4: **Take care of yourself.** Because your past can wear you down physically and emotionally, allow God to use your testimony fully by making a commitment to exercise and rest on a daily basis. Explore new and fun forms of exercise, such as kickboxing, spin class, or kayaking.

ACTION STEP 5: **Choose to focus forward.** Decide to trust that God has a plan to use your past for good in the future. Write out a formal declaration of trust; then sign and date it.

REFLECTION

Think about the following question as you read the rest of the book. We'll use your daydreaming about it in Tip 10: Capture Your *Live Big!* Dream.

Basic premises

- If you had assurance from God that He was thrilled with your plans to follow your dream and that He would not let you fail . . .

- If you had all the time and energy you needed . . .

- If the entire world were eager to support your vision with money and resources . . .

- If this were the ideal season of your life . . .

Specific premises in the five chapters so far

1. If you were free of all your fears . . .

2. If you truly had discovered the benefits and joy of exhaling . . .

3. If you honored your deepest longings . . .

4. If you knew for sure that you would persevere to the end of the race . . .

5. If you were healed of the wounds in your past and determined to let God use them . . . *what passionate,* Live Big! *dream would you pursue?*

Here's my answer to the reflection question. Hope it helps you dream!

If I were healed of the wounds in my past and determined to let God use them . . . I would launch a radio show and a syndicated newspaper column in which I was more open about my past, while doing LaserCoaching with those who are seeking to focus forward.

Prayer

God, I know that in all things, You work for the good of those who love You, for those who have been called according to Your purpose (Romans 8:28). Only You offer freedom, healing, hope, and a secure future. I thank You for how You planned, in advance, to turn all of my crises and problems into instruments for good—and that You have made that promise to all who believe in You. It gives me tremendous hope. I want to hold fast to You in the good times and the bad. I am grateful that You know my shortcomings and my strengths—and that You are willing to take me from where I am today. Help me always to know that You are my compassionate and caring Father. I give all my past hurt and troubles to You and ask You to put them to good use. In order to express my gratitude, I now choose to live my life completely sold out for You.

Expect Miracles

PERHAPS YOU'VE SEEN *Miracle on 34th Street,* A UNIVERSALLY loved Christmas movie. Have you ever wondered why this particular film has stirred so many hearts over the years? What is it about miracles that captivate our attention and draw us into the pulse of the story? Is it because they encourage childlike innocence that causes us to believe in happy endings? Is it the gift of hope they give us that we will find fulfillment in our journey? At least in part, one magical ingredient is that they showcase daily struggles that are transformed into success stories and new potential.

Wouldn't you be thrilled to see a miracle pop into your life today? Well, miracles occur more often than you probably realize. You see, a miracle is not all that complex or impossible in the grand scheme of God's design. True, a miracle is something beyond the ordinary. It's definitely a supernatural phenomenon. But miracles abound every day. The reason we don't see them is that we don't expect or ask for them. Let's step into the life of Mary Kay, a woman who experiences miracles in her life all the time.

Mary Kay is presently serving as a pastor at a nondenominational church and is launching a new part of her ministry as a writer. She has a zest for helping women know that they have value and that God has a wondrous plan for their lives. If you asked her about expecting miracles, she would sit down with you, share her story over a cup of coffee, and tell you about an awesome God who keeps His promises. I guarantee that her vivacious enthusiasm would rub off on you and that you'd find yourself expecting miracles, too!

> See, I have engraved you on the palms of my hands.
>
> Isaiah 49:16

Mary Kay was a "miracle baby," born premature and weighing only two pounds. Her father could hold her tiny body in the palm of his hand.

Nobody expected Mary Kay to survive. God, on the other hand, had distinct plans for His masterpiece! As Ephesians 2:10 helps us understand, she was God's workmanship *(poema),* created in Christ Jesus to do good works, which He prepared in advance for her to do. He must have whispered to her, "Live Big!" because her young life became a tremendous testimony to doctors, nurses, family, and friends that God is alive and that His purposes will stand.

Let's peek now at another marvelous miracle in Mary Kay's life. After living thirty wonderful years as a Catholic nun in a convent, she clearly sensed God calling her out into the world to serve Him in a different way. She felt certain that He wanted to enlarge her territory, as when "Jabez cried out to the God of Israel, 'Oh, that you would bless me and enlarge my territory! Let your hand be with me, and keep me from harm so that I will be free from pain.' And God granted his request" (1 Chronicles 4:10).

This would have been a decision of gargantuan proportions, bringing uncertainty and fear to anyone facing it, but Mary Kay was one who liked things particularly clear, organized, and safe. Frankly, after her fragile and tenuous beginning, she liked knowing that her future was secure. So, for her, this departure from the convent felt like leaping off a summit with no parachute. She had a choice: either to cling to her fear and stay where she was or to hold fast to her faith and plunge into the unknown.

She vividly remembers the morning she made her final decision. As she was once again praying over the matter, it was as if the Spirit of God lifted her onto her feet, and she heard herself declare: "OK, I'm going to stand tall and do this. I'm going to face this fear, because God has spoken to me."

Do you remember the Bible story about God speaking to Joshua, telling him to cross the Jordan River? "You [Joshua] and all these people, get ready to cross the Jordan River into the land I am about to give to them—to the Israelites" (Joshua 1:2). Well, that Scripture actually readied Mary Kay to expect miracles as she obeyed God's command. Soon she crossed over her own Jordan River with the blessing of the church and the loving support of her family and friends.

Six weeks after leaving a formal religious life, she was hired as director of religious education at a parish church, rented her first apartment, and bought her first car.

> All I have seen teaches me to trust the Creator for all I have not seen.
>
> Ralph Waldo Emerson[1]

Yet Mary Kay's greatest challenge and opportunity to expect a miracle loomed on the horizon, years away—and that chapter of her story begins as excitingly as had the first. One day, God graciously brought into her life a remarkable man named Kenny Moore. He became the love of her life and her best friend. They were inseparable and soon were happily married and serving God in their church. Mary Kay was ecstatic.

Then, seven and a half years later, all of that changed. In January 2003, she sat beside her husband in a doctor's office and heard the physician give the dreaded diagnosis: "Kenny, you have ALS, commonly known as Lou Gehrig's disease." As the doctor explained that Kenny had only two to five years to live, Mary Kay felt as if she'd been shot with a stun gun.

For months, she was like the walking dead, frozen in excruciating shock and grief. Feeling as though her heart had been ripped from her chest, she cried out to God with rivers of tears. *Why? Why him? Why me? Why now?* When her tears finally slowed from flowing on an hourly basis, she and Kenny made a commitment to celebrate each day as a gift from God. They chose as their special Scripture a verse from Deuteronomy: "Choose life, so that you and your children may live and that you may love the LORD your God, listen to his voice, and hold fast to him. For the LORD is your life" (Deuteronomy 30:19–20).

For the next three years, Mary Kay and Kenny held fast to the Lord and prayed for unending patience and unprecedented trust in Him. They asked for and believed that they would see a miracle in the form of physical healing, but God had a different plan. During her quiet time one morning, Mary Kay read these words by author Beth Moore: "Oh, friend, would you dare to believe that He is completely able? If He doesn't grant you what you ask in faith, it is never because He lacks the power. I believe it's because He wants to release an all-surpassing power and reveal an even greater glory through another answer."[2]

That insight caused Mary Kay to see things in an entirely different way and with a depth of faith she had never before experienced. For example, she had felt early on that she would not have the physical, mental, or emotional strength to get through this daunting trial. She had often felt utterly helpless, defeated, and afraid. Now she saw clearly the first of many miracles: The joy of the Lord became her strength and endurance. Each day, despite her growing fatigue, she found the inner resources to press on and to pour out still more love on her husband. She experienced the newness of God's mercy every morning and the blessings that could have come only from Him.

She observed another miracle as well: Even amid the daily deterioration and paralysis of her husband's body, his countenance seemed filled with light, and he spoke words of love and comfort to those around him. As if that were not enough of a gift, Mary Kay then had the privilege of witnessing the longed-for miracle of forgiveness and reconciliation between Kenny and some of his family members. And to this day, she is overwhelmed by the miracle of having a family and a church family in which so many people constantly reached out to her and her husband with prayer, cards, calls, meals, and visits. She sighs. "We would not have survived without them."

Kenny, a faithful servant of Christ, received his crown of glory on February 5, 2006. Mary Kay says, "There was a Miracle on Roosevelt Street the day my husband died. He did so with such grace that it gave unforgettable testimony to all who witnessed God still being glorified through his tired body."

What miracle do you need in your life? Is it in your finances, marriage, friendships, job, health, spiritual growth, ministry, schooling, or addictions? Your miracle is just around the corner, waiting for you. Your miracle may not be that your loved one is healed, your finances are fixed, or your marriage is mended. Your miracle may involve a change of heart or a life-changing lesson learned. The key is trust and expectancy. When we expect, hope for, and wait patiently for a miracle, our God shows us favor and displays His power in His special way and in His incredible timing.

Five Action Steps from Your Life Coach

God desires to enlarge your life with miracles to strengthen your faith and help you fulfill His dynamic purposes for your life. If you will identify the miracles you *want*, you can expect that God will provide all you *need* to do His will. As in Mary Kay's life, so also in yours, it's possible for miracles to happen every day. Expect them. Look for them. Thank God for them in advance. And be encouraged by following these five steps.

ACTION STEP 1: **Write out a bottom-line need in your finances.** For one month, thank God daily for His financial blessings and give cheerfully to your church. Then, don't be surprised when your financial needs are met in mysterious ways and you become more aware of the difference between your needs and your wants.

ACTION STEP 2: **Overcome a negative attitude.** Whenever a negative thought enters your mind, replace it immediately with a positive thought. (Remember that it takes twenty-one days to change a habit, so be patient with yourself.) Expect a miracle as you ask God to help you turn your negativity over to Him.

ACTION STEP 3: **Believe God and take Him at His Word.** When you are overwhelmed with a huge obstacle or an unbearable burden in your life, ask God to increase your faith for a miraculous outcome. Search the

Scriptures for verses that will encourage and strengthen you. Write them on sticky notes and post them somewhere, such as on a mirror, where you can read them several times a day.

ACTION STEP 4: **Live in daily gratitude.** Journal each day to record at least one thing you are grateful for—even if, at first, the only thing you can think of is that the day is over. Focus on the goodness of God and His miraculous blessings, thanking Him in advance for continuing to weave His presence, peace, protection, and provision into every situation.

ACTION STEP 5: **See miracles all around you.** Get up early and watch the sunrise. Stop and smell the flowers. Listen to the sound of the wind and the birds. Take a walk through the woods. Sit by a lake. Lie down and gaze at the stars at night. Miracles are everywhere. Take the time to experience them.

REFLECTION

Think about the following question as you read the rest of the book. We'll use your daydreaming about it in Tip 10: Capture Your *Live Big!* Dream.

Basic premises

- If you had assurance from God that He was thrilled with your plans to follow your dream and that He would not let you fail . . .

- If you had all the time and energy you needed . . .

- If the entire world were eager to support your vision with money and resources . . .

- If this were the ideal season of your life . . .

Specific premises in the six chapters so far

1. If you were free of all your fears . . .

2. If you truly had discovered the benefits and joy of exhaling . . .

3. If you honored your deepest longings . . .

4. If you knew for sure that you would persevere to the end of the race . . .

5. If you were healed of the wounds in your past and determined to let God use them . . .

6. If you were in the habit of always expecting miracles . . . *what passionate,* Live Big! *dream would you pursue?*

I love this reflection question!

If I were in the habit of always expecting miracles . . . I would ask God for the miracle of financial backers, a leadership team, and a variety of support staff so I could devote more of my time to shepherding our certified instructors.

Prayer

Faithful Father, I thank You that You are a God of signs, wonders, and miracles, even in modern times. Spur me on to expect and to look for miracles in my life, both big and small. I want to choose a life of blessings and purpose. I want to hold fast to You in good times and in bad. I want to cross my own Jordan River and know that the land of promise and expanded territory is a place for expecting miracles at every step. Increase my faith, Lord. Lead me and guide me in Your ways, so that I, too, can testify to Your power and goodness at work in my life. Amen.

Forgive Someone

CAN YOU RECALL A TIME WHEN YOU FELL SHORT IN YOUR relationship with someone and needed to be forgiven? Or a time when you were wronged by someone and had to make a decision to forgive the person or carry a grudge? These situations cause us to gravitate in one of two directions: healing and reaping the rewards of personal freedom or facing the damage of bitter resentment. These choices, when made repeatedly over time, determine whether we will live a life of sadness or joy, a life of regrets or God's best. Let's look at the story of Michelle, a woman who had such a choice to make.

For months, God had been drawing Michelle into closer communion with Him. As He revealed more of His character to her, she thanked Him for being her faithful guide. During that sweet season, she spoke at an out-of-state Christian women's retreat, delivering a powerful message about hope and unmerited forgiveness. She did not know that God was readying her to face a life-altering experience that would require her to walk the talk of what she had just shared with the women.

When Michelle arrived home, she was at a spiritual peak. Within minutes of setting her suitcases down, she noticed an unfamiliar number on her phone's caller ID. Upon investigation, she was devastated to learn that Harry, her husband of ten years, had been having a brief affair. The shock of his infidelity catapulted Michelle from her mountaintop experience to the pit of despair and disbelief. Several days later, in an honest attempt to begin the reconciliation process, Harry further confessed that it had been a yearlong affair. Michelle's life was turned upside down, and her decision about whether to forgive Harry would be determined by a series of earlier events.

Michelle had been born into a family of strong Christian heritage, surrounded by models of Christlike living. She accepted Jesus at a young age and grew in her walk with the Lord. After she left home for college, though, she quickly relegated God to a back burner, and an unbearable void soon developed in her life. To fill the emptiness, she had a string of promiscuous relationships, including with Harry, a young man who did not know the Lord and who, like her, was primarily interested in worldly pleasure.

Michelle began to distance herself from her parents to avoid feeling any condemnation. Occasional conversations with them inevitably turned to topics of a spiritual nature, so she became increasingly entangled in a web of lies and deceit. She grew hostile at the mere mention of Christ's love. Her parents knew that their precious, youngest child was self-destructing, yet any attempts by them to reach out to her were rejected. They clung to hope by a thread.

After eight years of the growing estrangement from God and her family, Michelle secretly married Harry. In one final act of defiance, she wrote a letter to her parents stating that by the time they received her letter, she would be married to and honeymooning with this man they had never met. They could take it or leave it, and frankly, she preferred that they would leave it.

The blow to these God-serving parents, as well as to Michelle's sister, was undeniably one of the lowest moments in their lives. The knowledge that she was closing the door to them and God was a crushing disappointment. Yet within a few short days, an outrageously hopeful idea began to grow in the hearts of Michelle's mom and dad, an idea for reconciliation that would require heavenly intervention.

Shortly after the newly married couple returned home from their honeymoon, Michelle's dad called them. When Harry answered the phone, he heard, "Hello, son, this is Michelle's dad. We love you both and want to fly you and your family here to meet our family."

This incredible, sincere act of grace melted the cold wall that had formed around Michelle's heart. She knew that she and Harry would be lavished with love, and that is precisely the reception they got. Her family's demonstration of unconditional acceptance had a profound, lifelong impact on Michelle, which caused her to ask them and God for forgiveness for her habitual wrongdoing. Harry was not as easily won over, yet this incomprehensible gift of forgiveness had planted a seed that might be harvested later.

After the reunion, Michelle grew in her relationship with God, but the unanticipated onset of her distinctly different lifestyle began to drive a wedge between her husband and her. "You are not the woman I married," he said, and Michelle wondered how she would ever endure the consequences of marrying a man who would not be the spiritual leader in their home.

The couple argued constantly and spent a great deal of time apart, as they no longer had any social activities in common. The resentment and guilt Harry felt were magnified when he was with Michelle, so he learned to avoid her. One day, when their relational chasm had grown to Grand Canyon proportions, Harry fled into the arms of another woman who said she liked him just the way he was.

After Michelle learned of the betrayal, she struggled through all of the emotions that swept over her, yet she continually felt God's presence. Biblically, she knew she was supposed to forgive her unbelieving spouse, since he had asked sincerely for forgiveness: "If a woman has a husband who is not a believer and he is willing to live with her, she must not divorce him" (1 Corinthians 7:13). But in her anger, she couldn't help contemplating divorce.

Based on Harry's repentance, her family urged her to attempt reconciliation. Michelle knew intuitively that her only hope was to focus on her experience with grace through her parents' unfathomable forgiveness, as well as God's merciful gift of salvation at the expense of His beloved Son. Jesus had died a selfless, undeserved death in order to grant her enormous favor. The parable of the prodigal son, as told in Luke 15:11–32, came to mind.

In that story, the father's clemency was not warranted, yet he welcomed his defiant, disobedient son home with open arms. This was Michelle's own story as well, in her relationship with her earthly parents and with her heavenly Father.

Shortly after learning of the affair, Michelle's cousin Nancy sent her an e-mail with this prayer from Ephesians: "To the praise of his glorious grace, which he has freely given us in the One he loves. In him we have redemption through his blood, the forgiveness of sins, in accordance with the riches of God's grace that he lavished on us" (Ephesians 1:6–8).

Those verses confirmed to Michelle that God had not only forgiven and redeemed her, but He had also lavished His grace upon her. She knew that forgiveness, as modeled by Christ, was her only option. She had to begin to see Harry through Jesus's eyes—as His child who had strayed—or there would be no hope left for their marriage.

> All of us in the church need "grace healed eyes" to see the potential in others for the same grace that God has so lavishly bestowed on us.
>
> Phillip Yancey[1]

She prayed and asked others to pray that God would work a healing miracle in both of them.

Michelle's thoughts were confirmed when she read Matthew 18:21–35, the poignant parable of a servant who was forgiven of his debt without condition of imprisonment or even a payment plan. His request for pardon had been granted by the king, yet this forgiven subject chose to deal harshly with a friend who owed him a much smaller sum of money. Because the servant disregarded the favor he had received, the king revoked his pardon: " 'Shouldn't you have had mercy on your fellow servant just as I had on you?' In anger his master handed him over to the jailers to be tortured, until he should pay back all he owed. This is how my heavenly Father will treat each of you unless you forgive a brother or sister from your heart" (Matthew 18:33–35).

It was clear that it was God's command for Michelle to forgive as she had so graciously been forgiven. But how could she ever forget Harry's disregard for their marriage vows? How could she move beyond her pain? She knew that forgiveness would need to be a conscious decision made moment by moment, but what could she do about the fact that godly forgiveness had to be grounded in love—a love she couldn't summon?

> God's forgiveness is one of His greatest acts of love toward us. He wants forgiveness to be one of *our* greatest acts of love toward others.
> Stormie Omartian[2]

Michelle chose to honor God by loving her husband, even though she still felt a great deal of lingering bitterness. As the

Holy Spirit enabled her, she took baby steps by doing small acts of kindness for this man who had hurt her deeply.[3]

Harry's response was an overwhelming desire to renew the close friendship he once had with his wife. This was the salve that began to heal Michelle's mistrust. She noted with astonishment that God placed in her heart the desire and ability to forgive her truly repentant husband, lovingly and fully. She knew it was God's gift to her. Lavishing mercy and grace on each other, although not an easy task for either Michelle or Harry, yielded more rewards than they ever could have imagined.

The once perplexing forgiveness Harry had received from Michelle's parents, and now received from her, helped him grasp the marvelous concept of redemption. Forgiveness not only brought about healing in their marriage as the couple began to fall in love again, but it also stirred a spiritual response in Harry. Seven months into the forgiveness process, during the Easter season, he prayed and asked God to forgive him for his sins and to come into his life.

Today, the acts of loving kindness and forgiveness from both God and family have built a powerful testimony that Harry and Michelle are able to share with others. The glory of God is manifested in their story loaded with examples of His infinite and matchless grace.

Michelle gives this loving advice to others who may be in a marriage relationship broken by adultery: "I don't want to mislead anyone who has been the victim of an affair to become a victim again by giving completely of herself without reciprocal effort. I was blessed to have a husband who was sincerely sorry, while you may be facing a very different reality. Although forgiveness is not optional, let the Holy Spirit be your guide in the details having to do with your well-being and healing."

Choosing to forgive and to be forgiven allows us to live large and fulfill the plans God designed specifically for us. The reward of surrendering anger, hurt, bitterness, self-pity, and mistrust is healing for the forgiver, if not also for the forgiven. Today would be a good day—actually, a great day—to forgive yourself or someone else or to ask for forgiveness.

Five Action Steps from Your Life Coach

Forgiveness is an act of surrendered obedience to God, as commanded in the Bible: "Forgive as the Lord forgave you" (Colossians 3:13). It is a willful, cognitive choice that often precedes the emotional response of feeling like forgiving someone. Pastor Rick Warren taught me that forgiveness is a process of "fake it till you make it." In other words, we make the decision to forgive; then we act our way into the feeling of forgiveness. Here are some proven steps regarding forgiveness for you to consider.

ACTION STEP 1: **Thank God for His forgiveness.** Look for scriptures detailing Jesus's sacrificial gift of forgiveness. Take special note of the lack of conditions placed on His forgiveness. Praise Him for this unconditional and unwarranted gift.

ACTION STEP 2: **Reflect on your own experience with grace.** Reflect on the many instances that God and others have granted you grace when you have fallen short. Journal the feelings you have about being the recipient of forgiveness, and express your gratitude to God—and to others when appropriate.

ACTION STEP 3: **Ask God to reveal any unforgiveness in your heart.** Write the name of someone who has hurt you. Note why you are hurt and/or angry. Ask God for grace to see that person through His eyes. Pray for the person's well-being and, if appropriate, speak to him or her about it. Then burn or shred the paper as a sign of turning the situation over to God.

ACTION STEP 4: **Choose to demonstrate forgiveness by action.** Where God has revealed an unforgiving attitude in your heart, choose to show His love by doing something kind for the person who has hurt or wronged you. Do it as an act of worship to your Redeemer.

ACTION STEP 5: **Forgive yourself.** Make a decision

to surrender any feelings of blame, guilt, or self-hate to God. Then ask the Lord to make you sensitive to any of these feelings that may rear their ugly heads in the future. Tell Him that you commit to surrendering them forevermore as you notice them.

REFLECTION

Think about the following question as you read the rest of the book. We'll use your daydreaming about it in Tip 10: Capture Your *Live Big!* Dream.

Basic premises

- If you had assurance from God that He was thrilled with your plans to follow your dream and that He would not let you fail . . .

- If you had all the time and energy you needed . . .

- If the entire world were eager to support your vision with money and resources . . .

- If this were the ideal season of your life . . .

Specific premises in the seven chapters so far

1. If you were free of all your fears . . .

2. If you truly had discovered the benefits and joy of exhaling . . .

3. If you honored your deepest longings . . .

4. If you knew for sure that you would persevere to the end of the race . . .

5. If you were healed of the wounds in your past and determined to let God use them . . .

6. If you were in the habit of always expecting miracles . . .

7. If you had lovingly forgiven yourself and everyone who ever hurt you—and you knew that you had been forgiven unconditionally by God and others . . . *what passionate*, Live Big! *dream would you pursue?*

This reflection question may make you pause in deep thought, but in the end, I hope you go for it! Here are my thoughts that were eye opening for me.

> *If I had lovingly forgiven myself and everyone who had ever hurt me—and I knew that I had been forgiven unconditionally by God and others . . . I would enjoy myself more by singing, laughing, and being less critical of myself. I would spend lots of time visiting the founders of our Life Coaching Centers around the world and teaching them this concept.*

Prayer

Lord, I am incredibly humbled by and grateful for the incomprehensible gift of forgiving grace that You granted me on the cross, even though I continue daily to fall short of who You created me to be. Help me, Jesus, to see my offenders through Your eyes. Grant me what I cannot attain by myself: a love for them and a desire to forgive them. Father, provide me with opportunities to lavish them with love. Thank You for this release from anger, hurt, and shame, which frees me now lovingly to fulfill the legacy You have crafted intentionally for me. Amen.

Eat Dessert First

D O YOU WORRY NONSTOP, THUS SQUELCHING ANY CHANCE of having any fun in life? Have you ever asked yourself these questions: How can I truly enjoy life? When will I stop fretting over endless details and start delighting in the present moment? What does it look like to live with no regrets? How can I make the most of every opportunity? If so, hold on tight while we talk about the fact that life's dessert is not meant to be saved but savored—sooner rather than later! Life is just too short not to eat dessert first. Today would be a perfect day to taste some of the sweetness of life that you've kept stored on a shelf for another day. Here's Joyce's story about how she learned to relish spontaneity and downtime, although she went kicking and screaming through her introductory course.

Joyce was introduced to Jesus Christ at the age of twenty. A friend invited her over for coffee and shared the wonderful truth that God loves her, that He has a plan for her future, and that this plan is explained in God's Word, the Bible. Joyce didn't hesitate to respond that day; she knew that she had been longing for something to help her make sense of her life. Later, as she began to read the Bible, she realized how far off course her lifestyle was from God's best. She asked Him for a like-minded friend to go to church with, pray with, and talk with about her newfound faith—preferably a nice guy! Shortly thereafter, an acquaintance from high school, Christopher Meekins, returned home from the navy. Chris had also recently trusted in Jesus as his Savior, and it wasn't long before they discovered they were both on the same spiritual journey.

Soon Chris and Joyce were married and started a family. With the birth of their first child came Joyce's new role as a mom. She had been an only child and had no idea what to do with a baby. She recalls standing beside her newborn son's crib and crying in exasperation, "Why won't you sleep?" The following years brought three more little ones.

The harried young mother of four drew much advice from older, more experienced women with knowing smiles and sincere wishes. Their words of wisdom echoed the same theme each time: "Oh, honey, enjoy your babies now. Time passes so quickly. Before you know it, your children will be grown. How I wish I had those days back!" Those pleas touched Joyce's heart. *They must have missed something major in their children's lives to talk this way,* she thought. That idea scared her, and she found herself constantly mulling over their words.

Along with having a family, Joyce loved working as a cosmetologist. Truth be told, the days she did stay home with kids and laundry were mind-numbing. What did she have to show for all of her efforts at the end of the day? Usually nothing. How could she escape this feeling of mediocrity? How could she live with more gusto?

As Joyce grew in her Christian faith and learned about the high value God places on marriage and motherhood, she sensed a shift in her priorities. If being a wife and a mother were important in God's eyes, maybe it was time to make a career change. She decided to quit her job and focus on becoming the best wife and mother she could be. What followed was some serious God-seeking, book-reading, class-taking, prayerful activity. She read what the apostle Paul had to say about the secrets to finding contentment, and she determined to apply them to her newly upgraded role: "Understand what the Lord's will is. . . . Be filled with the Spirit. . . . Sing and make music from your heart to the Lord, always giving thanks to God the Father for everything, in the name of our Lord Jesus Christ" (Ephesians 5:17–20).

Making the decision to embrace joy and gratitude was easy. Actually doing it proved to be much harder without surrendering fully to the power of the Holy Spirit. Joyce is a live-by-the-planner, Type A personality, whose philosophy was "Work now, play later." It was always a struggle for her to stop working and simply goof off. After all, if she spent time with her children doing the silly things described in parenting magazines, such as blowing seeds off a dandelion or watching ants clean up cookie crumbs, how could she justify the lost momentum to her work-flow?

As is often the case with couples, Joyce and her husband had opposite home-life philosophies. Though he was an excellent provider for his family, his motto was "Play now, work later"—or, as he likes to say, "Eat dessert first!" One gorgeous spring morning, Chris decided the family should go on an outing to the park and take advantage of the new warmth of the season. Joyce, on the other hand, had already decided that it was a perfect day to make a dent in all of the chores screaming to be done. Playtime could wait. Chris, being the thoughtful husband he is, told Joyce, "Well, you can stay home and work if you like, but the kids and I are going to the park. Have a nice time cleaning!"

At the last minute, wise woman Joyce made a defining choice that changed her life forever. You guessed it. She jumped in the car and had fun that day with her family, leaving the chores on the list. She recalls her thought process: "The mental gymnastics I did were Olympic-gold-worthy! I figured it from every angle and finally just gave in to my unwillingness to be left behind doing all the work." That experience led Joyce to make a promise to herself to be always on the lookout for those random, irreplaceable opportunities that never get written in a planner.

> It is not how much we have, but how much we enjoy, that makes happiness.
> Charles Spurgeon[1]

As God continued His heart-transformation work in Joyce, she actually began to delight in happenstance. She realized the benefits of serendipitous adventures with the people she loved. Newly aware of the privilege God had given her as a wife and mother, she was determined not to miss a moment of this precious time entrusted to her.

Now that Joyce's four kids are grown and on their own, God has opened the door to a different career for her, one that employs all of the wisdom of her mothering years. Joyce is the women's ministry director at her church as well as for her denomination's district of eighty-six churches. She has the privilege of contributing to many women's lives. Not surprisingly, she meets many who struggle to feel joy for various reasons (e.g., they still believe Satan's lies about them; they can't stop berating themselves for their poor choices; they're holding on to grudges; or they fear the future). Through her own experiences, Joyce's ministry has grown into helping women live the joyful truth of God's Word. Her keen desire is to see women set free to know Jesus, embrace joy, and discover the incomparable masterpiece—indeed, the magnum opus—that God created them to be. She loves to borrow a phrase from Esther 8:16: "It was a time of happiness and joy, gladness and honor."

Joyce tries to apply the "Eat dessert first" attitude in every area of her ministry. For example, before any business is discussed at her team's annual planning weekend, the women address one item of utmost importance at the top of the agenda: They play a wildly fun and highly competitive game of Spoons (a variation of Musical Chairs but with spoons). The lucky winner holds the coveted trophy for one full year. Why would Joyce begin a serious weekend of planning and seeking God with a nonsensical tradition of playing a game? It's her gentle reminder that time passes too quickly not to take time first to play, bond, relax, and laugh (aka, eat dessert first!) with the people with whom you do life!

It took Joyce years to translate this mindset to her own self-care habits, but now she is consistent in remembering to breathe deeply, smile, dance, and sing whenever she feels like it. In fact, she's been known to go completely off-schedule and allow herself a nature walk, nap, bubble bath, ice-cream sundae, musical interlude, or girlfriend giggle. These rewards are like minivacations that inspire and invigorate her. She confesses, "I now place such high value on these times of extravagant refreshment that I don't know how I ever functioned without them. I must have been wound up really tight!" (To which Chris playfully chimes in, "Amen to that!")

> My advice to you is not to inquire why or whither, but just to enjoy your ice cream while it's on your plate.
>
> Thornton Wilder[2]

It can be difficult for us to think about Jesus, the son of God, laughing and having a good time. Yet He modeled living in the moment when parents brought their children to Him. Do you remember the story in Mark 10:13–15, when Jesus's disciples tried to send the kids away, but He rebuked the disciples, saying, "Let the little children come to me"?

I can picture Jesus eagerly welcoming the little ones, cherishing the delightful gift of spending time with them and inviting them to be the focus of His attention. I can imagine His laughter as He gently bounces a toddler on His knee and whispers a prayer that ends with a light kiss on the child's head.

> Joy is prayer—Joy is strength—Joy is love— Joy is a net of love by which you can catch souls.
>
> Mother Teresa[3]

Joyce and Chris recently celebrated their thirtieth wedding anniversary, and not only does Joyce savor her time with her husband and adult children, but she is at peace as she looks back over her mothering years. She attributes this joy to the decision made years earlier to eat dessert first. She encourages us: "The busy-ness never ends! Make memories with your loved ones and with those who need your unconditional love. And, by the way, even if you are alone for the day and have not accomplished a thing yet, stop and serve yourself a generous portion of your favorite, God-approved reward. It will tickle you."

Five Action Steps from Your Life Coach

Is it hard for you to take the time to play? Is your spirit heavy with to-do lists? Is joy only an occasional experience for you? Don't delay another minute! Give all your cares to Jesus, and get a fresh start today. Stop to treasure the little blessings He sends and to celebrate the gifts He has placed within your reach.

Check out the suggestions below to reignite your smile. You may laugh as you stop to realize that your dreams are unfolding before your eyes.

ACTION STEP 1: **Just do it.** Give yourself permission to eat dessert first. Have some fun. Take out your planner and cross off what was written for this afternoon or this evening or one day soon. In that time slot, go to a park, see a movie, read a book, or window-shop—anything you like (as long as it's unproductive). Then go a step further and plan some goof-off time at least once a week, in addition to your Sabbath day.

ACTION STEP 2: **Literally eat dessert first.** If the thought of ruining your appetite is upsetting to you, it may be a clue that someone other than Joyce is wound a bit too tightly. Loosen up! Go to your favorite restaurant and order dessert first. It really makes perfect sense calorie-wise, because you'll then be too full to order an appetizer, salad, entrée, and soda! Think of it as a weight-loss plan.

ACTION STEP 3: **Consider your view of God.** Is it hard for you to picture Jesus smiling? Do you think of Him as a stern taskmaster? Recall how John refers to himself in his gospel as "the disciple whom Jesus loved" (John 13:23; 19:26; 21:7, 20). Then nickname yourself "the disciple whom Jesus loves," because you truly are. Ask God to reveal His smile to you on an hourly basis for an entire week.

ACTION STEP 4: **Embrace joy.** Imagine that your life values are listed in priority order, from most important at the top to least important at the bottom. Do discipline, responsibility, and work ethic dominate the top of your list? Where does joy sit? Now, let ten simple joys float into your mind, such as smelling a baby's hair, feeling the warmth of the sunshine on your face, cuddling a kitten or puppy, making snow angels with kids, or writing poetry. Set about to experience such joys often.

ACTION STEP 5: **Be surprised by the moment.** Get ready, in the next seven days, to be surprised and to create some of your most treasured memories. If a neighbor waves while you're outside gardening, start a conversation. If your kids are playing a game, join in. If a co-worker invites you to go to lunch, go! If your husband or boyfriend wants to go to the park, drop everything, jump in the car, and don't look back. You'll be a changed woman.

REFLECTION

Think about the following question as you read the rest of the book. We'll use your daydreaming about it in Tip 10: Capture Your *Live Big!* Dream.

Basic premises

- If you had assurance from God that He was thrilled with your plans to follow your dream and that He would not let you fail . . .

- If you had all the time and energy you needed . . .

- If the entire world were eager to support your vision with money and resources . . .

- If this were the ideal season of your life . . .

Specific premises in these eight chapters

1. If you were free of all your fears . . .

2. If you truly had discovered the benefits and joy of exhaling . . .

3. If you honored your deepest longings . . .

4. If you knew for sure that you would persevere to the end of the race . . .

5. If you were healed of the wounds in your past and determined to let God use them . . .

6. If you were in the habit of always expecting miracles . . .

7. If you had lovingly forgiven yourself and everyone who ever hurt you—and you knew that you had been forgiven unconditionally by God and others . . .

8. If you were in the habit of eating dessert first, of enjoying life to the fullest . . . *what passionate,* Live Big! *dream would you pursue?*

I say "no holds barred" on your answer to this last reflection question! Here's mine:

If I were in the habit of eating dessert first, of enjoying life to the fullest . . . I would buy season passes to the theater with a group of girlfriends— or, better yet, I would start to date and let a man buy the season passes!

Prayer

Loving Father, thank You for joy! I am sorry that I often forget how precious and powerful it is. Open my eyes to the blessings that surround me. Empower me to use the gifts of relaxation, creativity, and inspiration to follow my dream. Teach me to smile broadly, laugh deeply, and love wholeheartedly. I want to be more like You, dear Lord. Thank You for never being too busy to talk to me and for always being happy to hear my voice—even though I have not accomplished anything to merit Your love. Amen.

PART 2

· · · · · · · · · · · ·

Your Time to Dream Large and Passionately

Ask Jesus for Vision

Y OU'VE READ THE TRUE STORIES OF EIGHT INCREDIBLE women who have braved life and learned some of the secrets of Living Big. They are everyday saints in my eyes because they're running the race to win the prize of Christ Jesus. As women who lead surrendered lives, they are primed to fulfill God's calling—and I consider it a high privilege to be on their cheerleading squad.

One of their secrets to . . .

- survival,
- success,
- significance, and
- surrender

. . . is that they continually ask Jesus to open their eyes to the truth and what they need to see. They are not shy about praying for insight regarding their daily circumstances and long-range plans.

I would be doing you a great disservice if I did not hit the pause button now and devote some attention to that eye-opening behavior. Understanding a biblical model for how to gain vision, wisdom, discernment, truth, and knowledge—and doing some practice exercises—will revolutionize how you discover and fulfill your distinctive life purpose. Let's read the story of one unlikely man, the blind beggar Bartimaeus, who has a lot to teach us on this topic of asking Jesus for the ability to see what needs to be seen. Mark 10:46–52 tells us:

> They came to Jericho. As Jesus and his disciples, together with a large crowd, were leaving the city, a blind man, Bartimaeus (which means "son of Timaeus"), was sitting by the roadside begging. When he heard that it was Jesus of Nazareth, he began to shout, "Jesus, Son of David, have mercy on me!"
>
> Many rebuked him and told him to be quiet, but he shouted all the more, "Son of David, have mercy on me!"
>
> Jesus stopped and said, "Call him."
>
> So they called to the blind man, "Cheer up! On your feet! He's calling you." Throwing his cloak aside, he jumped to his feet and came to Jesus.
>
> "What do you want me to do for you?" Jesus asked him. The blind man said, "Rabbi, I want to see."

"Go," said Jesus, "your faith has healed you." Immediately he received his sight and followed Jesus along the road.

The Prayer of Bartimaeus

I can't wait to meet Bartimaeus when I get to heaven, so I can thank him for teaching me to be bold in my prayer requests. Hearing the blind beggar's story changed my life. I now constantly use what I call the Prayer of Bartimaeus whenever I'm in desperate need of answers. When Jesus asks me, "What do you want me to do for you?" I reply, "Teacher, I want to see the truth about———" (and I fill in the blank). I have shared this prayer with many others because I know that spiritual sight and insight are worth more than gold in all situations.

Here are just a few of the blindnesses people have been healed of after faithfully praying the blind man's prayer. They've told me, "I asked for my eyes to be opened to the truth about———" (and they fill in the blank). "And then the truth set me free." For example:

- how to manage my finances
- how to move forward in pursuit of my godly dreams
- why I get depressed so easily
- which of my character faults needs addressing
- when to consider developing a new relationship
- how to handle office gossip and politics
- what to do about my sugar addiction

- what my next step is for spiritual growth
- what words to use to apologize to someone
- how to "march through" a fear I have
- what ministry God has planned for me
- and more!

Some others who have prayed to see truth have been so overwhelmed by the answers they received that they've said to me, "I don't want to see anything else now! I've seen too much already." I simply tell them to take a break for a while to get their courage back, so they'll be able to see what God would like to reveal to them next.

The more I thought about this prayer, the more I realized that its power is simply in the fact that we're taking the time to listen and respond to Jesus when He talks to us. Yes, when the Creator of the World and Ruler of the Universe asks us a question, I think He really expects and appreciates an answer.

> If you then, though you are evil, know how to give good gifts to your children, how much more will your Father in heaven give the Holy Spirit to those who ask him!
>
> Luke 11:13

God is our heavenly Father, and He's just waiting to send us His Holy Spirit as our counselor and teacher who will guide us into all wisdom.

Let's take a closer look, behind the scenes, at how Bartimaeus got what he asked for—how he got what he wanted and needed: his sight and a new lease on life.

The Bartimaeus Story

The gospel writer Mark begins his story with Jesus and His friends leaving Jericho and heading out on a long trek to Jerusalem. Bartimaeus, a blind beggar clothed in filthy, torn, smelly rags, squats beside the road. He had been going about his daily routine of begging for food and money when he heard that Jesus of Nazareth was nearby. Because Bartimaeus couldn't see, he had to rely on his keen sense of hearing to decipher the truth amid all the ruckus.

> *Do you need to fine-tune your hearing to decipher the truth amid all the ruckus?*

He cried out, "Jesus, Son of David, have mercy on me!" (Mark 10:48). As a Jew, Bartimaeus was actually calling out to the long-awaited king that his people believed would restore Israel to its physical and spiritual prominence. He was asking the great, God-sent, earthly leader to help him. Mark's Christian readers had a hindsight advantage, because they knew that the Son of David was also the Son of God, who had gone to the cross, died, been resurrected, and redeemed them. The blind Jewish man, though, only understood that a righteous, mortal king—who could rescue him—was nearby.

The text indicates that some people yelled at the beggar, telling him to be quiet. Disregarding the warnings of the crowd, Bartimaeus shouted all the louder to the Son of David to have mercy on him. He was a man of persistence and perseverance, wasn't he? He was begging for pity; he was claiming the physical healing that was part of the Messianic blessing. As a Jew, he had the right to appeal to the Son of David for favor; a Gentile did not.

Then an incredible thing happened. The Son of David, who was heading to the City of David (Jerusalem) to begin his intense and deadly passion journey, stopped to talk to this blind man. Pastor Tom Holladay, my supervisor at Saddleback Church years ago, once explained to me that the original text meant that Jesus had His "jaw set firmly" on Jerusalem, that He was moving steadfastly toward His crucifixion. There would be no turning back for Jesus, yet He took time to talk to a dirty beggar who had only a sketchy and misdirected perception of who He was. Jesus said, "Call him." That's verse 49 in Mark's story, the beautiful "call" passage where Jesus beckons the man to come to Him.

The people called to the blind man, telling him to cheer up and get up. Bartimaeus threw aside his outer garment—some commentators say it was his bedroll. Regardless, we see it as a symbol that Bartimaeus knew he would be granted a second chance in life and would not need his previous encumbrances.

Do you also remember the "call" story of Simon and his brother Andrew, who immediately left their fishing nets behind (Matthew 4:18–20); of James and John, who left their father, Zebedee, in the boat (Matthew 4:21–22); and of Levi, who left his tax collector's booth (Luke 5:27–28)? When Jesus called them, they immediately left behind their old lives, anything that could have held them back.

> *What are you willing to throw aside or leave behind*
> *to meet with Jesus?*

Mark says that Bartimaeus jumped up and went to Jesus. This indicates that he sprang up at once, that he was eager to respond to the invitation, and that he obeyed with a sense of anticipation.

> *Do you have a sense of anticipation*
> *before you talk with Jesus?*

Then Jesus asked him: "What do you want me to do for you?"

> *Would you like Jesus to ask you that question?*

Bartimaeus humbly said, "Rabbi, I want to see." He was addressing Jesus in a reverential way because he knew he was speaking to a respected *Rabbouni,* which in Greek means "my Teacher, my Lord, my Master."

> *Like Bartimaeus, do you have a well-thought-out answer*
> *ready to give your Lord? Can you verbalize the most*
> *sincere prayer of your heart, the deepest desire of your soul?*
> *Will you tell Jesus right now what you need?*

Then Jesus said, "Go your way. Your faith has healed you." The emphasis here is on faith, on the fact that Bartimaeus believed Jesus would heal him. And because the word *healed* can also mean "saved," there's a double meaning: healed physically and saved spiritually.

When you pray for something, do you have Bartimaeus-sized, expectant faith that you will receive it?

The story ends with this sentence: "Immediately he received his sight and followed Jesus along the road" (Mark 10:52). That's a great summary of the message of this passage: that all who are blind can see Jesus and choose to follow Him. In fact, the technical term for "seeing Jesus" is *salvation,* and the term for "following Jesus on the way" is *discipleship.* So in this one brief account, we have a vivid picture of conversion and discipleship. At first, we see a blind beggar sitting beside the road; then we see a sighted man following Jesus down the road!

Would you like to see and follow Jesus?

Praying Expectantly for Sight and Insight

Pray the Prayer of Bartimaeus often. (Photocopy the prayer as printed on page 116, or write your answers directly on that page, or go to my ministry Web site to download my gift of a beautiful template that you can personalize and frame.) As you pray, ask

Jesus to send the Holy Spirit to give you insight into particular areas of your life. Ask Him to heal your blindness and open your eyes, granting you vision, clarity, wisdom, discernment, truth, knowledge, and focus. Ask Him to prepare your heart as you move away from deliberate blindness toward the path to which He is calling you, both daily and long-term. And pray for the ability to handle the truth that He reveals to you, because it's not always easy to deal with the truth or to obey what we're told to do.

Prayer of Bartimaeus

⤳✣⤳

Mark 10:46–52 personalized for you

They came to _____ [your city]. As Jesus and his disciples, together with a large crowd, were leaving the city, a blind woman, _____ [your first name], ("daughter of _____ [your parent's name]"), was sitting by the roadside begging. When she heard that it was Jesus of Nazareth, she began to shout, "Jesus, Son of David, have mercy on me!"

Many rebuked her and told her to be quiet, but she shouted all the more, "Son of David, have mercy on me!"

Jesus stopped and said, "Call her."

So they called to the blind woman, "Cheer up! On your feet! He's calling you." Throwing her cloak aside, she jumped to her feet and came to Jesus.

"What do you want me to do for you?" Jesus asked her.

The blind woman said, "My Teacher, Lord, and Master, I want to _____

_____

[your request]."

"Go," said Jesus, "your faith has healed you." Immediately she received her sight [in this area] and followed Jesus along the road.

Here are some sample requests for sight and insight that you may want to insert into the prayer if you have a hard time answering Jesus's question, "What do you want me to do for you?"

- I want to be free from all my fears. Open my eyes to Your almighty power, which conquers fear.
- I want to experience the freedom of exhaling. Let me clearly see several new habits You want me to develop now that will help me to breathe more deeply.
- I want to honor my deepest longings. Give me a bird's-eye view of the steps You want me to take today.
- I want to persevere to the end of the race. Take away my short-sightedness and escort me to the finish line.
- I want to heal from the wounds of my past. Give me insight into how You can use my past, and make me whole again.
- I want to expect miracles. Turn a spotlight on all the miracles I fail to see; fill my heart with gratitude for each one.
- I want to forgive and be forgiven. Help me to see the truth of Your unconditional love for me and for others.
- I want to start enjoying life by eating dessert first. Heal my blindness and help me to see and seize moments of joy. And let the fun begin today!

- I want to discover and fulfill my life purpose. Reveal Your plan to me, and open doors so I can realize Your vision for my life.

Keep a log of each blindness in your life that has been healed. The list of miracles and blessings will amaze you!

Capture Your *Live Big!* Dream

Wнат's a gal to do now?

Simply this: Remember that God Almighty created you with everyday, ordinary purposes—and also with a unique, more far-reaching purpose. He cares deeply about your next steps toward His glorious plan. Ask Him to prompt you to follow the coaching tips and take the action steps outlined in this book toward living the large, passionate life He has always had in mind for you. If you take one solid step toward Living Big for God, you will find that the rest of the commitments will follow naturally, a lot like dominos falling.

But in all fairness to you, I must take a moment to warn you about something. I guarantee that the road will get rocky at times, because life will continue to happen! And I can also assure you that Satan will not want you to pursue your God-inspired dreams. Let me give you a few examples of what has happened to me in the last thirty days of writing this book. I won't know until I get to heaven how much of it was simply because we live in a fallen world of human commotion and how much was the enemy trying to thwart God's plan.

Crazy Happenings While on a Mission to Finish This Book

- Credit-card fraud in seven locations—while the card was still in my wallet.
- Luggage lost for thirty-six hours, with my laptop battery inside.
- Flat tire on one of the busiest days of my life.
- Numb hands that wouldn't work without electrodes zapping them.
- Crashed computer and printer (totally my fault for plugging in a wrong cable).
- Virus on a loaner computer (I blame this one on computer demons).
- Corroded water heater, which left me with no hot water for five days, thus forcing me to shower at the community pool rather than bothering my neighbor during a holiday season.
- A tire bouncing off a car on the freeway breaking my

sunroof at 4:30 A.M., during the rainy season, while I was rushing to catch a flight.

- Sitting through a two-day jury-selection process for an armed-robbery case while 175 potential jurors were interviewed out of a pool of 200 (I was number 176, so I was not called).
- Physically and emotionally helping my son's family move to Colorado and concurrently helping my daughter move to another county in California.

All of this happened as I continued to run my ministry, teach at Rockbridge Seminary, and try not to overdo it after two back surgeries. I share this with you in an effort at full disclosure of what you may be signing up for when you move out, in faith, to accomplish what God has had in mind for you all along. You have to want your dream to come true so intensely that, with God's help, you can weather any storm that comes your way. In fact, you may decide to pray for what my friend Chaundel calls a "holy amnesia"—that God will help you forget all of the bad, discouraging, and frustrating stuff that happens.

Now that the fair warnings are out of the way, we have just three things left to do together in this coaching session. The first is to discuss a decision you need to make regarding your future, by looking at two options for dealing with your life purpose. The second is to get your "*Live Big! Dream & Plan*" in a concrete, written form. And the third is to make your "*Live Big!* Keepsake Scrapbook.*"

We'll start by looking at your two options:

OPTION 1: Make decisions that attract your life purpose.

OPTION 2: Make decisions that sabotage your life purpose.

I think it might help to see your choices further laid out in opposing lists, as in the table here.

Two Options for Dealing with Your Life Purpose

Option 1: Attract It	Option 2: Sabotage It
Face your fears.	Be a scaredy-cat.
Learn to exhale.	Hold your breath, waiting for the other shoe to drop.
Honor your deepest longings.	Do nothing, but be jealous of others living your/their dream.
Use your past for good.	Drag debilitating regrets into your future.
Forgive someone.	Be a prisoner to bitterness and/or hate.
Eat dessert first.	Deprive yourself of simple rewards and moments of joy.

Does it help to see your options in such a stark, clinical comparison? As your Life Coach, I have confidence in you, confidence that with the help of the Holy Spirit, you will choose Option 1 and begin to attract your life purpose more diligently.

Next, we will take a peek at your answers to the reflection questions in Part 1: What passionate, *Live Big!* dream would you pursue?

I already shared my answers with you in each chapter so you wouldn't be shy when you formulated your own responses while progressing through the book. Now, I'd like to show you how to put together all of your answers to create your *"Live Big! Dream & Plan."* Make sure you use present-tense language, as if you already are living your dream. Here's a sample.

Katie Brazelton's *Live Big! Dream & Plan*

I am having the time of my life as a radio personality and syndicated newspaper columnist on the topic of life purpose, and I also take time to dance, date, play, sing, and laugh more. I live in a small, private cottage (with additional guest rooms available to me, as needed) at our debt-free, one-hundred-acre international training facility, which is run by our world-class board of directors, leadership team, and support staff. I'm starting to write a manuscript, which I know to be my life's work, and I have approved a screenplay about a woman's angst and search for purpose. I oversee the training and spiritual development of our instructors and inspire them to fulfill their *Live Big!* dreams. And

I travel around the world encouraging the founders and staff of each of our two hundred Life Purpose Coaching Centers.

Three action steps I feel God leading me to take

1. I will start my own BlogTalk Internet radio show in the next month and do LaserCoaching with guests who call in.
2. I will go with my friend Jeannie to her ballroom dance class next week to check it out.
3. I will make an announcement in our next ministry newsletter that we are praying for an architect to donate two renderings of our hundred-acre campus.

☑ I further commit to adding new action steps as I complete these!

Katie Brazelton   _January 1, 2010_
Signature   Date

Now it's your turn to see your own *"Live Big! Dream & Plan"* in writing, so let's get busy doing that. Grab a piece of lined paper or write directly on page 125, or go to my ministry Web site to download a great template to use for this exercise.

_____**'s *Live Big!* Dream & Plan**

Describe your *Live Big! Dream & Plan* in first person, present tense, as if you are already living your dream.

Three action steps I feel God leading me to take

Write out your action steps, using specific details and a timeline.

1.

2.

3.

☐ I further commit to adding new action steps as I complete these!

_____   _____
Signature   Date

The last thing I get to do in our time together is help you create a chart of our journey; a photo collage of our adventure together. This "Keepsake Scrapbook" will help you remember what you wrote. My sample is printed here.

Katie Brazelton's *Live Big!* Keepsake Scrapbook

For your own scrapbook page, you can grab a piece of paper and divide it into eight sections, write/draw in this book on page 129, or you can go to my Web site to download a frameable template that you can use for this exercise. Fill in the eight blocks with a few key words and rough sketches from your narrative description. When you're done, put this and your narrative description where you will see them often and be reminded to pray about your dreams, hopes, and aspirations, which God has given specifically to you.

_____'s *Live Big!* Keepsake Scrapbook

Well, it's time to say good-bye now, and I don't want to leave without telling you that it has been my pleasure being your virtual Life Coach. I consider it an honor and a precious calling on my life. I would love to hear from you, so come visit me at my Web site (www.LifePurposeCoachingCenters.com/LiveBig).

As you embark on this wonderful journey, I want to offer a blessing on the pursuit of your *Live Big!* dream. May the Scriptures that I selected for you and pray constantly be a reminder to keep your eyes on God, who holds your future in His hands. May you surround yourself with family, friends, prayer warriors, at least one accountability partner, a church family, a Bible study group, a network of like-minded ministry people, and a Christian Life Coach to keep you on track. God bless!

Jabez cried out to the God of Israel, "Oh, that you would bless me and enlarge my territory! Let your hand be with me, and keep me from harm so that I will be free from pain." And God granted his request.

1 CHRONICLES 4:10

Then I heard the voice of the Lord saying, "Whom shall I send? And who will go for us?" And I said, "Here am I. Send me!"

ISAIAH 6:8

May he give you the desire of your heart and make all your plans succeed. May we shout for joy over your victory and lift up our banners in the name of our God. May the LORD grant all your requests.

PSALM 20:4–5

Many are the plans in a human heart, but it is the LORD's purpose that prevails.

PROVERBS 19:21

How to Contact the Author

To learn more about Katie Brazelton, PhD, MDiv, MA, bestselling author, Life Purpose Coach, and founder of Life Purpose Coaching Centers International (LPCCI), and her dream of continuing to open Life Purpose Coaching Centers worldwide, contact her at:

> Life Purpose Coaching Centers International
> P.O. Box 80550-0550
> Rancho Santa Margarita, CA 92688
> Info@LifePurposeCoachingCenters.com
> www.LifePurposeCoachingCenters.com

To invite Katie to give a life-changing keynote speech (with her special touch of humor) to your organization, contact:

> Ambassador Speakers Bureau in Tennessee
> Naomi@AmbassadorSpeakers.com

LPCCI is accredited by the International Coach Federation (ICF) and the International Association of Continuing Education Training (IACET) to conduct online and on-site coach-training classes for men and women. Katie has been a featured guest on radio and television broadcasts, such as *Midday Connection* and *100 Huntley Street.* She has had more than sixty articles published in the last few years in publications such as *Today's Christian Woman, Extraordinary Women,* and *Alive!* She has been honored to speak at such venues as Focus on the Family, as well as the American Association of Christian Counselors' World Conferences. Currently, she is a professor at Rockbridge Seminary, but she served previously as a licensed minister at the purpose driven Saddleback Church in California. She has two adult children, a daughter-in-law, and two grandsons. Check out Katie's Purpose Series books:

Pathway to Purpose for Women (paperback: 978-0-310-29249-4)

Pathway to Purpose for Women (audio CD: 978-0-310-26505-4)

Pathway to Purpose for Women (audio download: 978-0-310-26857-4)

Praying for Purpose for Women (paperback: 978-0-310-29284-5)

Conversations on Purpose for Women (spiral-bound: 978-0-310-25650-2)

Conversations on Purpose for Men E-Book and *Coed EZ-Forms* (available at www. LifePurposeCoachingCenters.com)

Character Makeover (paperback: 978-0-310-25653-3)

How to Learn More about the Women in *Live Big!*

For more specifics about the Life Purpose Coach professionals who shared their testimonies, visit www.Life PurposeCoachingCenters.com/LiveBig.

Tip 1: Face Your Fears—Darlene Lund

Tip 2: Learn to Exhale—Kristi Olson

Tip 3: Honor Your Deepest Longings—Judy Grandstrand

Tip 4: Don't Ever Give Up—Jamie Beran

Tip 5: Use Your Past for Good—Natasha Swanepoel

Tip 6: Expect Miracles—Mary Kay Moore

Tip 7: Forgive Someone—Michelle Cabell

Tip 8: Eat Dessert First—Joyce Meekins

Notes

TIP 1

1. Charles Stanley, *The Blessings of Brokenness: Why God Allows Us to Go through Hard Times* (Grand Rapids, Mich.: Zondervan, 1997), 22.

2. Henry Cloud and John Townsend, *Boundaries: When to Say Yes, When to Say No to Take Control of Your Life* (Grand Rapids, Mich.: Zondervan, 1992), 265.

TIP 2

1. Judy Garland, quoted in Karen Weekes, *Women Know Everything! 3,241 Quips, Quotes, and Brilliant Remarks* (Philadelphia: Quirk Books, 2007), 228.

2. John and Stasi Eldredge, *Captivating: Unveiling the Mystery of a Woman's Soul* (Nashville: Thomas Nelson, Inc., 2005), 179.

TIP 3

1. "Henry Thoreau Quotes," http://www.quotedb.com/quotes/2098.

2. "Mark Twain Quotes," http://www.en.thinkexist.com/quotes/mark_twain/.

TIP 4

1. Speech at Harrow School, Harrow, England, October 29, 1941. *Winston Churchill: His Complete Speeches*, 1897–1963, ed. Robert Rhodes James, vol. 6, p. 6499 (1974)

2. From Internet site: http://www.ordinarypeoplecanwin.com/dalecarnegie

TIP 5

1. Anne Graham Lotz, *My Jesus Is Everything* (Nashville, Tenn.: Thomas Nelson, 2005), 73.

2. Judith Couchman, *Designing a Woman's Life: A Bible Study and Workbook* (Sisters, Ore.: Multnomah Books, 1996), 91.

TIP 6

1. Ralph Waldo Emerson, *The Works of Ralph Waldo Emerson* (London: George Bell and Sons, 1904), 360.

2. Beth Moore, *Jesus the One and Only* (Nashville, Tenn.: LifeWay, 2000), 110.

TIP 7

1. Phillip Yancey, *What's So Amazing about Grace?* (Grand Rapids, Mich.: Zondervan, 1997), 175.

2. Stormie Omartian, *The Prayer That Changes Everything* (Eugene, Ore.: Harvest House, 2004), 238.

3. Visit http://www.LifePurposeCoachingCenters.com/Live Big for specifics related to forgiveness in the case of adultery.

TIP 8

1. From Internet site: http://www.brainyquote.com

2. From Internet site: http://www.quoteoftheday.wordpress.com

3. From Internet site: http://www.quotationspage.com